THE PROFESSOR'S SECRET
TO SURVIVING STATISTICS:

SPSS GUIDE & TUTORIAL

by
Dr. Jim Mirabella

First Edition

ISBN: 978-1-300-71143-8

DEDICATION

This book is dedicated to my wife, Karen, and my son, Sean. They are the loves of my life and my driving force, and they provide endless support to me. I am truly blessed with my family, my job, and all the gifts that God has given me.

TABLE OF CONTENTS

CHAPTER 1: ENTERING DATA

SPSS (PASW) is a
powerful statistical
package. It certainly
helps to have a basic
knowledge of statistics
when using the package,
but you will need to know
the basics of working with
the program before you
can even begin to explore
the many analytical tools
available. Let's begin by
opening SPSS.

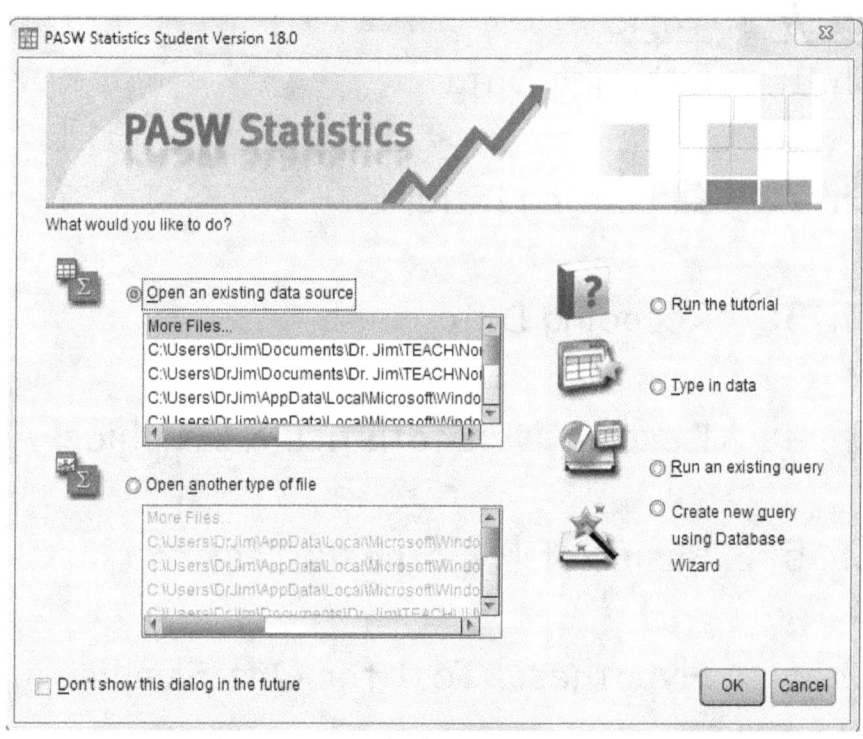

You will automatically see a pop-up asking what you would like to do. Most of the time you
will either OPEN AN EXISTING DATA SOURCE or TYPE IN DATA. Let's choose TYPE
IN DATA and OK.

The bottom of the screen shows two tabs: DATA VIEW and
VARIABLE VIEW. The DATA VIEW displays the raw data in
columns, with one column per variable. The VARIABLE VIEW
contains the definitions and formatting information of each
variable in the data set. You are currently in the DATA
VIEW. Since we are setting up a file from scratch, let's click
on VARIABLE VIEW.

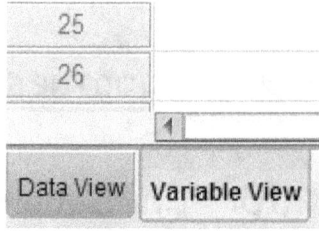

	Name	Type	Width	Decimals	Label	Values	Missing	Columns	Align	Measure	Role
1											
2											
3											
4											
5											

Here you see the many columns of the VARIABLE VIEW. Each row is a variable
completely defined. Let's set up a file for all students in a university's doctoral program.
Suppose we wanted to capture data that includes one's School, Gender, Age, home State,
Track number (i.e., an indicator of credits earned, sort of like Freshman / Sophomore /
Junior / Senior, but using # 1 – 3), and annual Income.

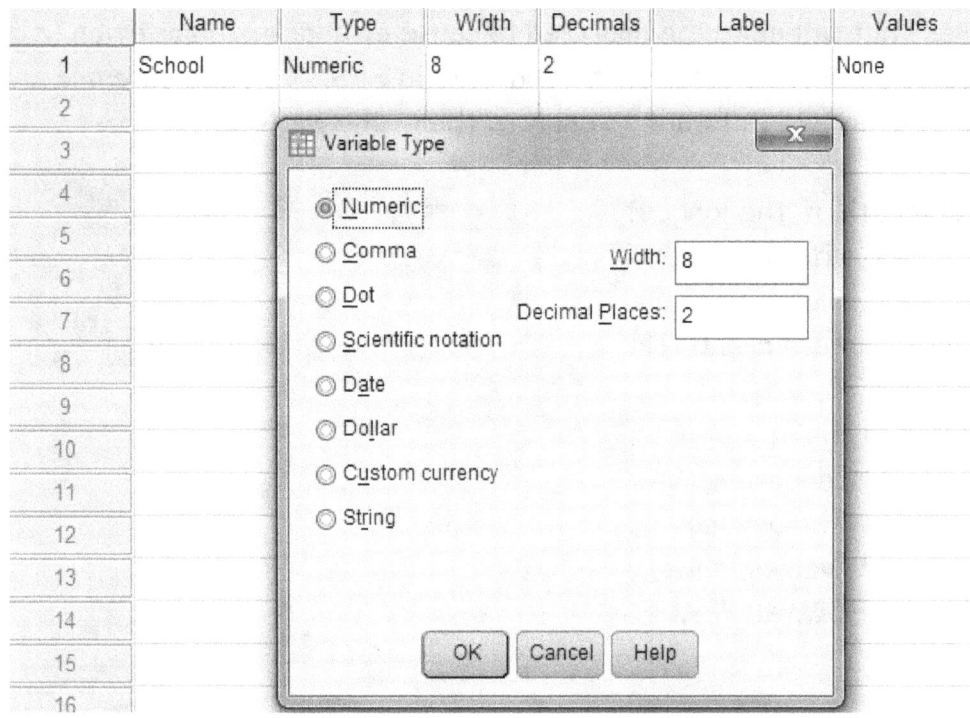

	Name	Type	Width	Decimals	Label	Values
1	School	Numeric	8	2		None

Enter <u>School</u> as the first variable name. Note that variable names can be as long as 64 characters, but must begin with a letter, and may not contain blanks. Try not to use very long names since it wastes space in the column display (as you will see later). The TYPE will automatically be populated with NUMERIC as the default. Click on the gray box with the 3 dots in it and the VARIABLE TYPE window pops open. There are eight options here:

- ➢ NUMERIC: this is a variable whose values are numbers.
- ➢ COMMA: this is a numeric variable with commas added for every three digits (i.e., separating thousands from millions from billions…, as in 1,234,567.89)
- ➢ DOT: this is similar to Comma except in European notation, dots are used as we use commas and commas are used as we use dots. For example, 1,234,567.89 in the USA would appear as 1.234.567,89 in Europe.
- ➢ SCIENTIFIC NOTATION: this is a numeric variable expressed with the leading digit followed by decimal values and multiplied by 10 to a power. For example, 1,230,000 would become 1.23×10 to the 6th power (written as 1.23E+6).
- ➢ DATE: this is a numeric variable in one of several date / time formats.
- ➢ DOLLAR: this is a numeric variable expressed as currency, with a dollar sign in front, and commas separating every third variable.
- ➢ CUSTOM CURRENCY: this is a numeric variable expressed as currency which is formatted in a unique manner.
- ➢ STRING: this is a non-numeric variable and is not used in any calculations. It may contain any characters.

School can be entered as a STRING or as NUMERIC. It is recommended that STRING be reserved for variables that will never be analyzed because of a lack of repetition (e.g., student's names) because STRING data cannot be analyzed in SPSS. Since there are only four schools to choose from and we will want to analyze them, choose NUMERIC.

The WIDTH is the total length of the longest possible value in the data set, with decimals included. For example, if the longest possible value is 1,234,567.89 you would use a WIDTH of 9 and DECIMAL PLACES of 2. At this university, there are only Schools of
(1) Business & Technology, (2) Education,
(3) Human Services and (4) Psychology, so School can only have 4 possible values; thus, let's use a WIDTH of 1 and DECIMAL PLACES of 0. Then click OK.

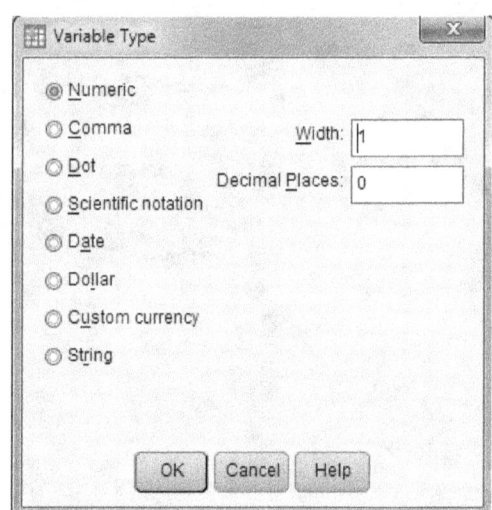

	Name	Type	Width	Decimals	Label
1	School	Numeric	1	0	Learner's School

The LABEL provides an opportunity to give a lengthier variable name with spaces and special characters if needed. If a LABEL is used, then all statistical output will substitute that label in place of the variable name; otherwise the variable name will be used. It is wise to take advantage of this function as much as possible. Here I used "Learner's School", but use whatever makes sense to you.

Click on the gray box under VALUES and a pop-up window will appear. Here we define the values that will be used for School. Let's assume 1 = Business & Technology, 2 = Education, 3 = Human Services, and 4 = Psychology.

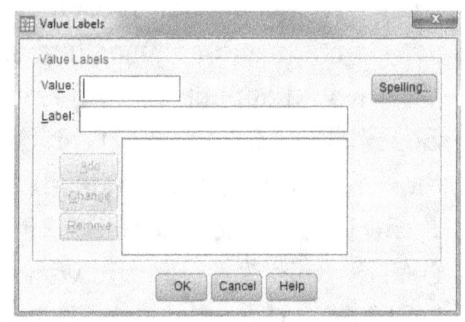

Put "1" in the VALUE box and "Business & Technology" in the Label box. Click ADD. Then repeat for the other three schools.

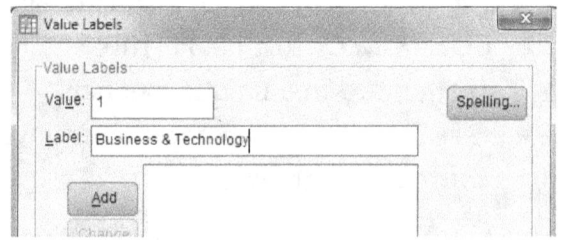

When entering the raw data, use only 1-4 for the schools as specified here. This will allow us to do analysis on this variable AND all statistical output will automatically substitute the name of the school for the numbers that are entered. It also makes it easier to enter data and then translate from a single digit number into a lengthy character string as desired. Now click OK when done.

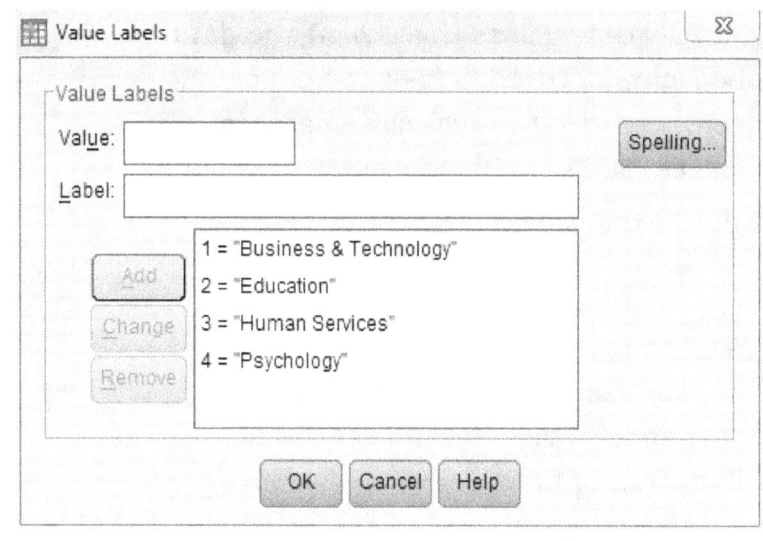

.

The next column is MISSING. Here you enter values in the data set which indicate the value is missing. If you are manually entering data, you can merely leave missing data blank, but if you import data from a database, it is possible that the system encodes a value like -99999 when a value is missing, and you would need to input the system values so SPSS knows how to treat them. Since we are manually entering data, you can just skip this part.

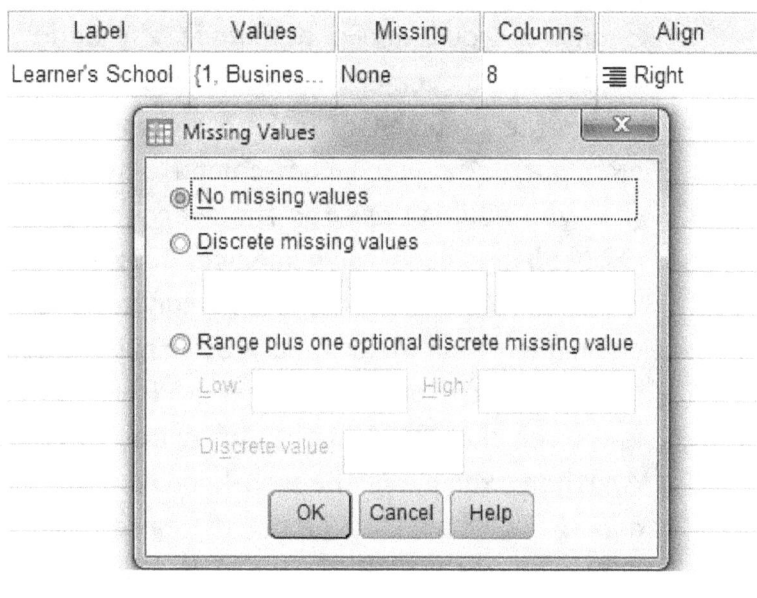

COLUMNS is merely the physical width of the column as displayed in the DATA VIEW. You could change the size here or you can change it by going to the DATA VIEW and dragging the lines that separate the columns.

If your variable name is very long, you will need to make the column extra wide just to display the complete name, which is why brief variable names are best.

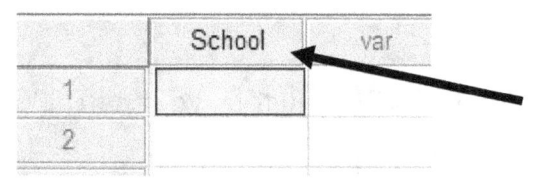

ALIGN determines if you want the data to be right-justified, left-justified, or centered. This is typically a personal choice, but sometimes convention dictates the format.

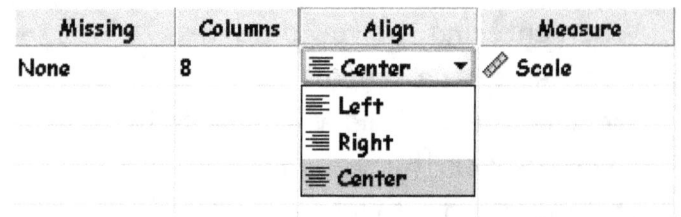

MEASURE is critical because different measurement types use different statistical tools. You will see three different options.

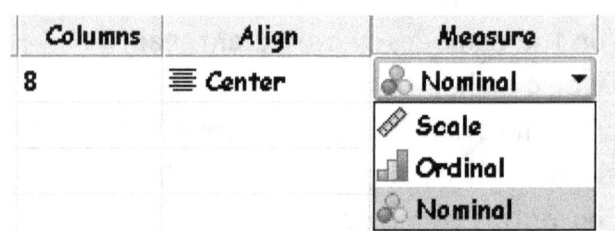

> NOMINAL is used for categorical data. Any numbers here cannot be used for anything beyond counting. Even numerical data here cannot be used analytically. Examples would be Gender, Race, Zip Code. <u>School</u> is clearly nominal, even though we are using numbers 1-4 for the data. The numbers are meaningless in their values (i.e., you cannot make a judgment about a value of 4 being larger than 2, for example). And you cannot compute averages or other statistics on nominal data (i.e., you wouldn't ask for the average zip code of your class).
> ORDINAL is used for numerical data with an order of magnitude. Typically data which is ranked fits here. You can make comparisons about numbers being larger or smaller than others, but you cannot judge how far apart they are. For example, if rankings are used for order of finish in a race, 1st place is better than 2nd which is better than 3rd, but the differences between the positions are not consistent. Another example is the well-known Likert Scale in which 5 = strongly agree, 4 = agree, 3 = neither agree nor disagree, 2 = disagree, 1 = strongly disagree → a rating of 4 is clearly higher than a 2, but you cannot state that it is twice as good, as the gap from a 1 to a 2 may be gigantic, while the gap from a 2 to a 3 might be small. Here you are limited in the statistics that can be computed, but there are some which can be done (mainly nonparametric statistics).
> SCALE data accounts for the rest. This includes data which can have any statistical analysis performed on it. Here the magnitude of the numbers is a factor and the differences between values are consistent. Variables such as <u>Salary</u> and <u>Age</u> fit the bill, for a dollar is a dollar, and a salary of $40k is twice as much as $20k.

	Name	Type	Width	Decimals	Label	Values	Missing	Columns	Align	Measure	Role
1	School	Numeric	8	0	Learner's School	{1, Busines...	None	8	Center	Nominal	Input

For the ROLE, just leave it as INPUT. Now we have a variable completely defined. Let's do the rest.

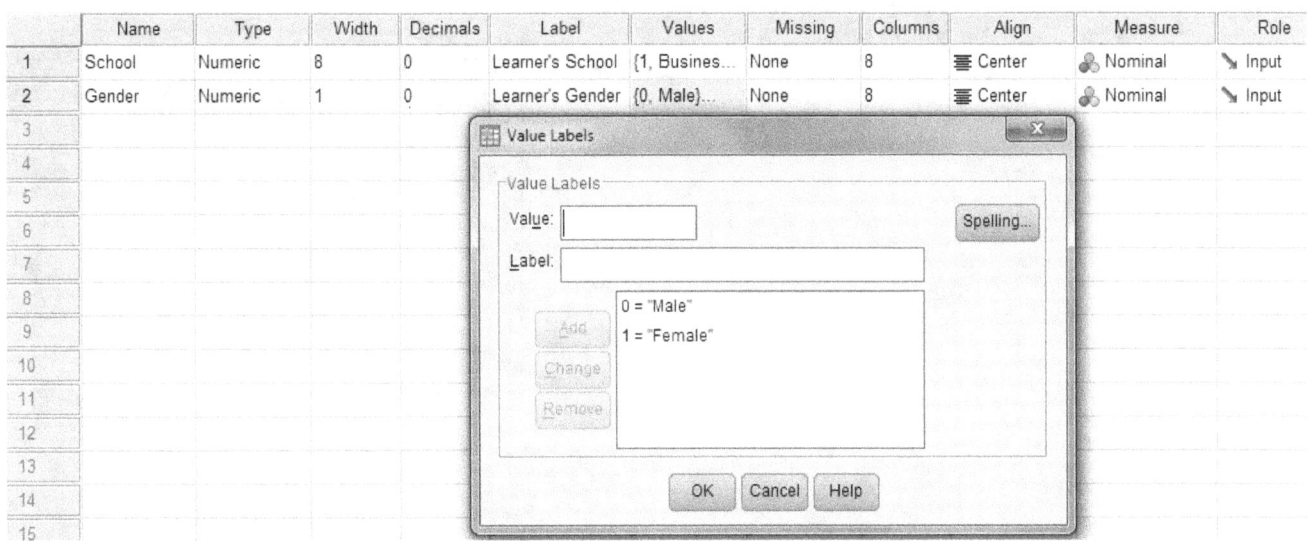

	Name	Type	Width	Decimals	Label	Values	Missing	Columns	Align	Measure	Role
1	School	Numeric	8	0	Learner's School	{1, Busines...	None	8	≣ Center	🔵 Nominal	⬦ Input
2	Gender	Numeric	1	0	Learner's Gender	{0, Male}...	None	8	≣ Center	🔵 Nominal	⬦ Input
3											
4											
5											
6											
7											
8											
9											
10											
11											
12											
13											
14											
15											

Gender should be set up similarly to School except that the LABEL is "Learner's School" and the VALUES have only two possibilities with 0 = Male and 1 = Female. You could even add a third if you wish (e.g., 2 = Unknown) since some responses are left blank on surveys to keep from disclosing personal info.

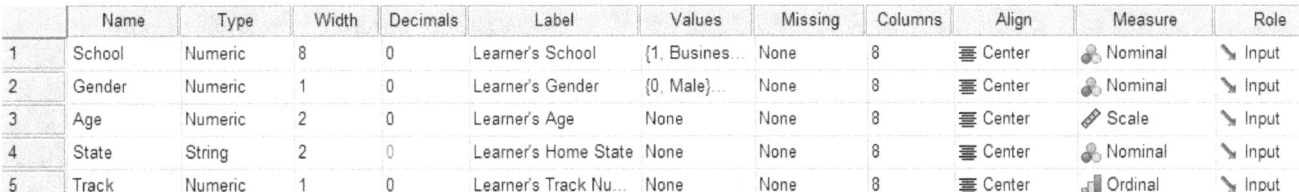

	Name	Type	Width	Decimals	Label	Values	Missing	Columns	Align	Measure	Role
1	School	Numeric	8	0	Learner's School	{1, Busines...	None	8	≣ Center	🔵 Nominal	⬦ Input
2	Gender	Numeric	1	0	Learner's Gender	{0, Male}...	None	8	≣ Center	🔵 Nominal	⬦ Input
3	Age	Numeric	2	0	Learner's Age	None	None	8	≣ Center	📏 Scale	⬦ Input
4	State	String	2	0	Learner's Home State	None	None	8	≣ Center	🔵 Nominal	⬦ Input
5	Track	Numeric	1	0	Learner's Track Nu...	None	None	8	≣ Center	📊 Ordinal	⬦ Input

Age needs a WIDTH of 2 since ages will clearly go into double digits. The LABEL is "Learner's Age" and there is no need for VALUES since we are not replacing a number with a string (what you enter is the real age). The MEASURE is SCALE in this case.

State is a STRING variable. If you choose to spell out the State, you need to be able to fit names as large as "North Carolina", but if you use postal abbreviations, then you only need two characters (which I will use here). Change the LABEL to "Learner's Home State."

Track is a numeric variable with only three possible values → 1, 2 or 3. Since the numbers are the track numbers, there is no need to use VALUES to translate (unless you want the statistical output to display "Track 1" instead of just "1"), which is a personal choice. The LABEL could be "Learner's Track Number". The MEASURE is ordinal because Track 1 is earlier than Track 2 which is earlier than Track 3, but there is no consistency in the gaps between the track numbers.

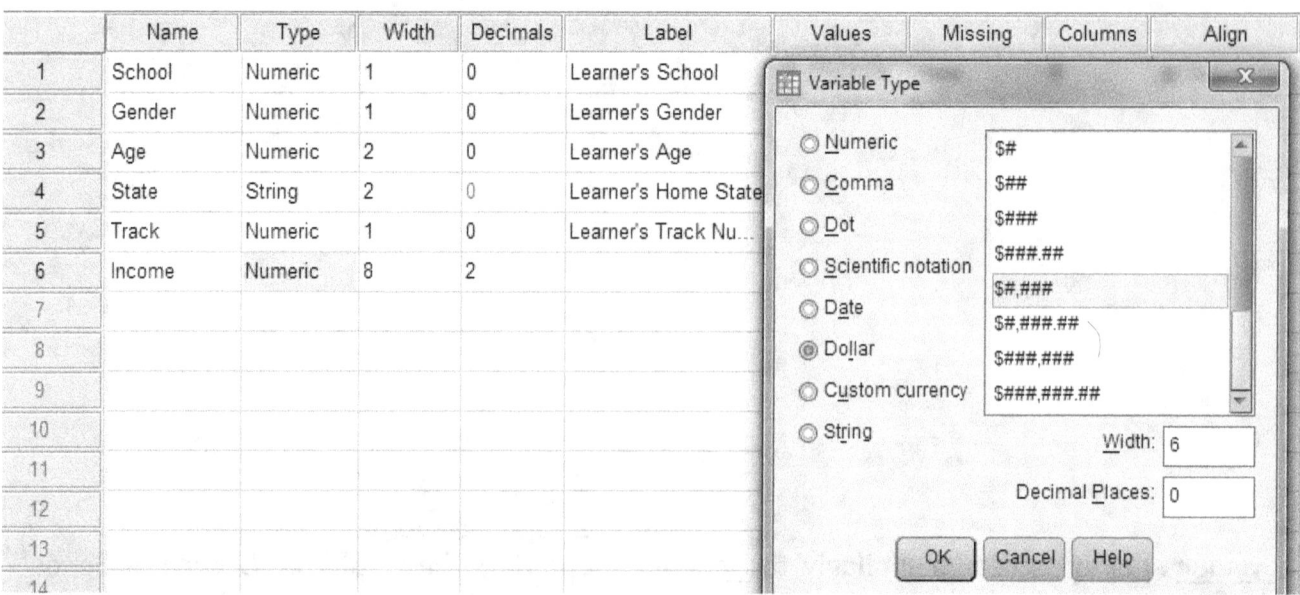

Income is a numeric variable which is a dollar value. It can be formatted in many ways. You may have the actual income in dollars, in thousands of dollars, or you might have the income in ranges (e.g., $20-30k, $30-40k, etc.). Let's go with the actual income in dollars.

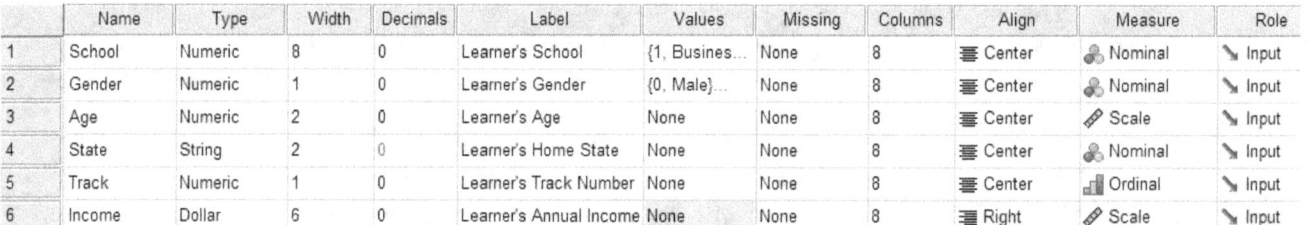

Income is also a Scale variable. Change the LABEL to "Learner's Annual Income". And VALUES don't make sense to use for SCALE data. You now have the setup complete and it is time to enter raw data. Go to the DATA VIEW.

	School	Gender	Age	State	Track	Income
1	1	0	35	FL	3	$80,000
2	1	1	43	GA	2	$70,000
3	1	0	51	AL	1	$75,000
4	1	1	29	CO	2	$65,000
5	2	0	44	FL	3	$55,000
6	2	1	55	MN	2	$60,000
7	2	0	37	TX	1	$50,000
8	3	1	60	TX	2	$55,000
9	3	0	30	FL	3	$45,000
10	4	1	40	MN	2	$40,000

Now you can enter data, making sure to follow the setup rules. So if the first learner was a 35-year old Track 3 male from Florida with an income of $80k who is from the School of Business & Technology, you would enter the data as shown above in row 1.

Save the file by going to
FILE → SAVE AS.

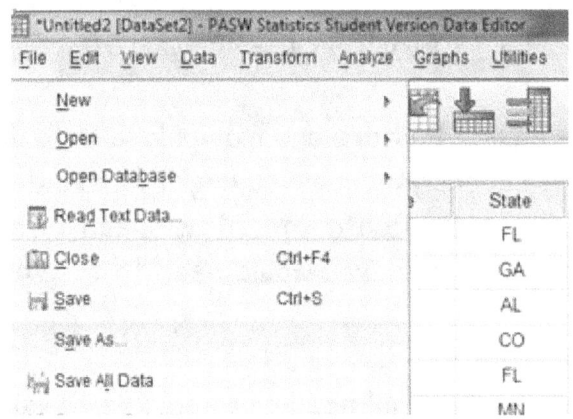

Then give it an appropriate
name and click SAVE. In this
example, I used the file name
COLLOQUIA ATTENDEES.sav.

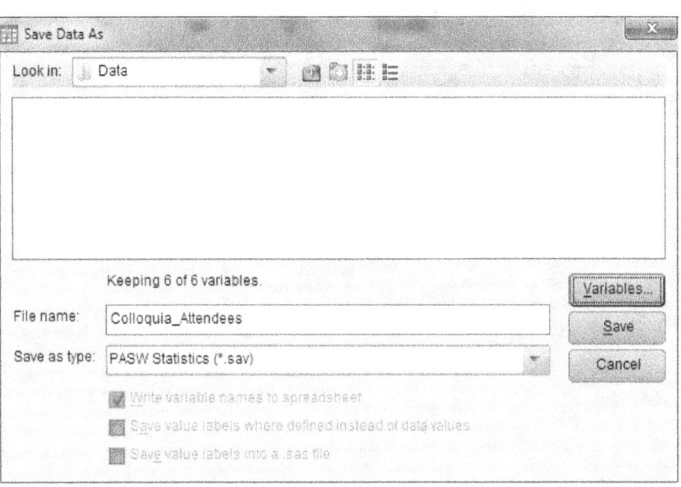

You may click on VARIABLES if you
wish; then you will see a pop-up
asking which variables you want to
keep in the file. You have the
option of deselecting some of them
for whatever reason and then
CONTINUE. Note that the
Student Version of SPSS will force
you to eliminate variables if you
have more than 50 in the file.

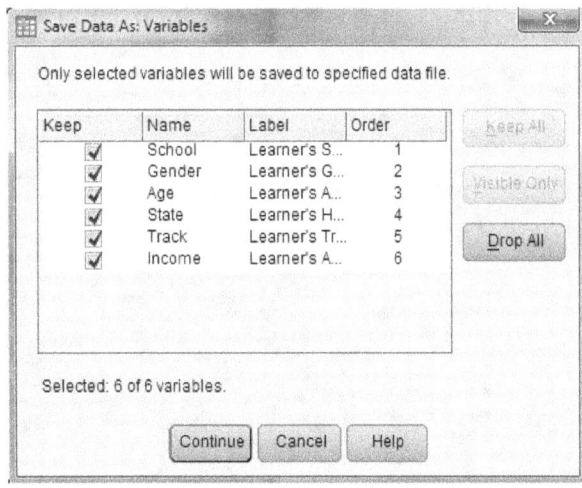

If you are happy with your variables, then click on SAVE to finalize the process. And
with that, you have now set up and saved a data file. It is highly recommended that you
save early and save often. You should save the file as soon as you set it up, and
throughout the process of loading data, as you wouldn't want to start over.

CHAPTER 2: IMPORTING DATA

Often it is easier to store and manipulate data in MS Excel until you are ready to begin your statistical analysis. Or you might have a database with employee or student data and be able to export data into a few specific formats, such as text or Excel (but rarely SPSS). In either case, you would need to take advantage of SPSS's ability to import data.

Before we begin, we will need an Excel file to work from. Suppose we have a file named GRADES.xls which looks as follows: (you can create it easily yourself or download it from www.drjimmirabella.com/spss).

	A	B	C	D	E	F
1	Name	Profile_YN	Track	Exam_40pts	Term Paper_50pts	Participation_10pts
2	Abby	1	3	38	48	10
3	Bob	0	2	40	45	9
4	Chloe	1	1	32	40	8
5	David	1	2	35	50	9
6	Ellie	0	1	36	35	7
7	Frank	1	1	24	30	8
8	Gretchen	1	3	28	42	10
9	Hank	0	2	40	49	7
10	Irene	1	1	33	38	9
11	Justin	1	1	36	40	10

Now let's import the file (make sure you have the Excel file closed first).

With SPSS open, go to FILE →
OPEN → DATA.

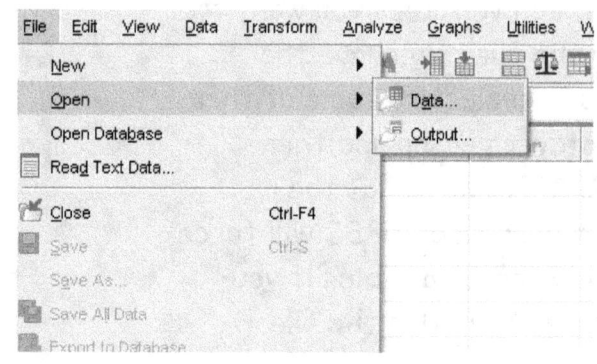

Change the FILES OF TYPE to "Excel (*.xls)" from the drop-down list.

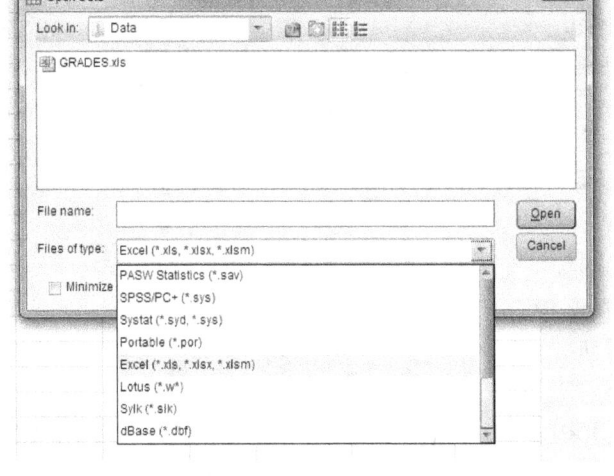

Select the file to import (in this case, GRADES.xls). Then click on OPEN.

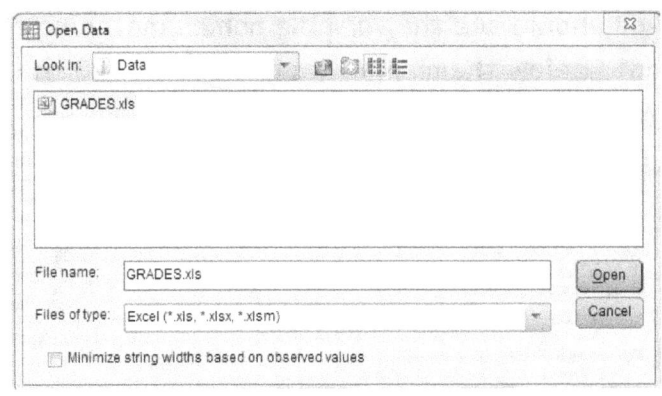

Next a window will pop up asking for the WORKSHEET and RANGE to import. It defaults to SHEET1 (the first worksheet in the file) and the entire range of values. Note the checked box with "READ VARIABLE NAMES FROM THE

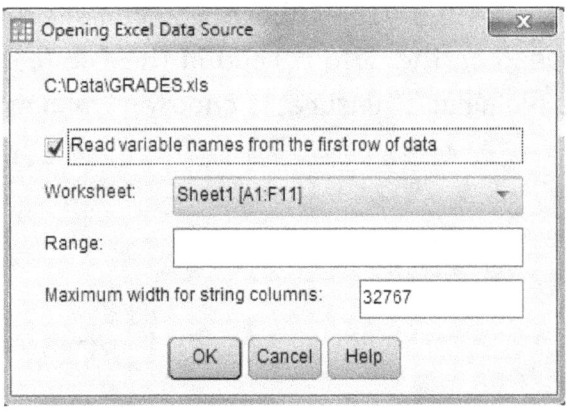

FIRST ROW OF DATA"; since the first row of data in our Excel file contains the variable names, leave this checked. Since we want the entire file imported, you needn't enter a range (just leave it as is to get all of A1:F11). Now click CONTINUE. Select the file to import (in this case, GRADES.xls). Then click on OPEN.

	Name	Profile_YN	Track	Exam_40pts	Term_Paper_50pts	Participation_10pts
1	Abby	1	3	38	48	10
2	Bob	0	2	40	45	9
3	Chloe	1	1	32	40	8
4	David	1	2	35	50	9
5	Ellie	0	1	36	35	7
6	Frank	1	0	24	30	8
7	Gretchen	1	3	28	42	10
8	Hank	0	2	40	49	7
9	Irene	1	1	33	38	9
10	Justin	1	1	36	40	10

SPSS opens up in the VARIABLE VIEW (below) where we can edit the setup of the variables.   It is possible it may open in the DATA VIEW (above) depending on your setup, and you should see the variable names matching the first row of the Excel file and all of the data below them. Now we need to set up the variables, so go to the VARIABLE VIEW.

	Name	Type	Width	Decimals	Label	Values	Missing	Columns	Align	Measure	Role
1	Name	String	8	0		None	None	8	Left	Nominal	Input
2	Profile_YN	Numeric	11	0		None	None	11	Right	Unknown	Input
3	Track	Numeric	11	0		None	None	11	Right	Unknown	Input
4	Exam_40pts	Numeric	11	0		None	None	11	Right	Unknown	Input
5	Term_Paper...	Numeric	11	0		None	None	11	Right	Unknown	Input
6	Participatio...	Numeric	11	0		None	None	11	Right	Unknown	Input

In the VARIABLE VIEW above, you can see the settings were automatically chosen by SPSS based on the data it read in the file (e.g., if it sees characters anywhere, it chooses Nominal, if unsure, it chooses Unknown). Let's make some adjustments.

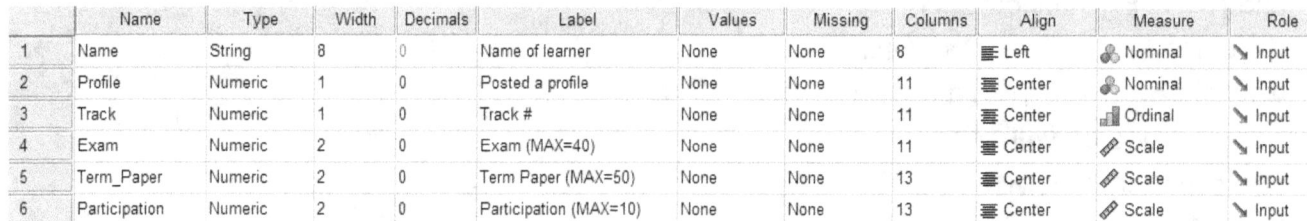

	Name	Type	Width	Decimals	Label	Values	Missing	Columns	Align	Measure	Role
1	Name	String	8	0	Name of learner	None	None	8	Left	Nominal	Input
2	Profile	Numeric	1	0	Posted a profile	None	None	11	Center	Nominal	Input
3	Track	Numeric	1	0	Track #	None	None	11	Center	Ordinal	Input
4	Exam	Numeric	2	0	Exam (MAX=40)	None	None	11	Center	Scale	Input
5	Term_Paper	Numeric	2	0	Term Paper (MAX=50)	None	None	13	Center	Scale	Input
6	Participation	Numeric	2	0	Participation (MAX=10)	None	None	13	Center	Scale	Input

Now we have better LABELS for the charts and graphs. Also, the WIDTHS of each variable were adjusted to fit the largest possible number to be entered. Profile was changed to NOMINAL since it is a Yes / No response. Track was changed to ORDINAL per the example explained in Chapter 1. Exam, Term Paper and Participation scores were changed to SCALE. I also simplified the variable names just to keep the columns trim, but that is entirely optional and purely cosmetic.

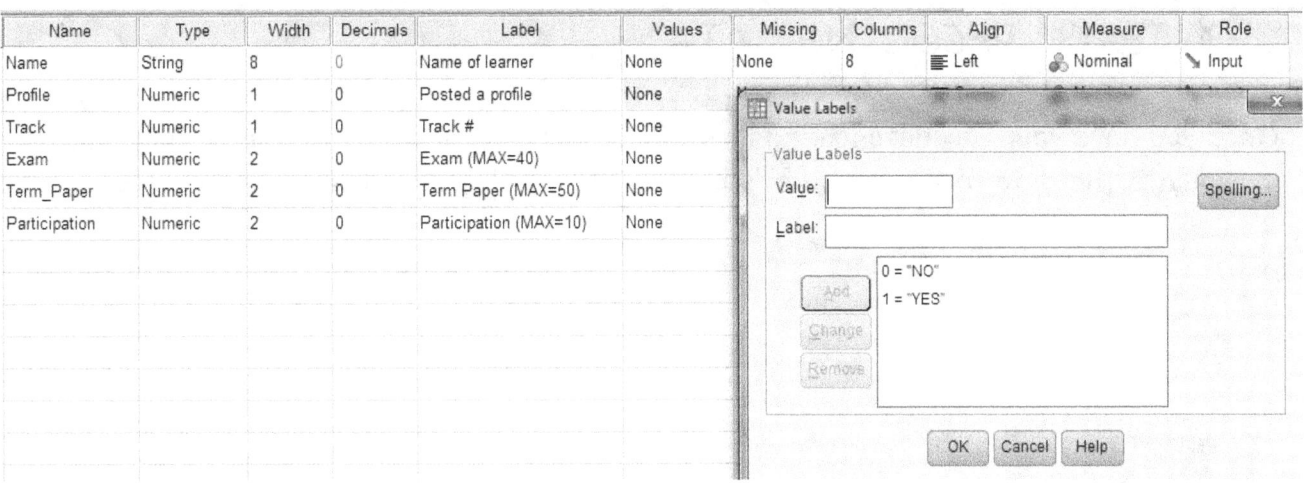

Name	Type	Width	Decimals	Label	Values	Missing	Columns	Align	Measure	Role
Name	String	8	0	Name of learner	None	None	8	≣ Left	Nominal	↘ Input
Profile	Numeric	1	0	Posted a profile	None					
Track	Numeric	1	0	Track #	None					
Exam	Numeric	2	0	Exam (MAX=40)	None					
Term_Paper	Numeric	2	0	Term Paper (MAX=50)	None					
Participation	Numeric	2	0	Participation (MAX=10)	None					

As for VALUES, <u>Profile</u> has a value of 0 for "No" and 1 for "Yes", so we need to add those accordingly.

	Name	Profile	Track	Exam	Term_Paper	Participation
1	Abby	1	3	38	48	10
2	Bob	0	2	40	45	9
3	Chloe	1	1	32	40	8
4	David	1	2	35	50	9
5	Ellie	0	1	36	35	7
6	Frank	1	1	24	30	8
7	Gretchen	1	3	28	42	10
8	Hank	0	2	40	49	7
9	Irene	1	1	33	38	9
10	Justin	1	1	36	40	10

The only last touch you should make is to adjust the COLUMN SIZE to suit you (it is strictly for display purposes). Rather than change the COLUMN size in the VARIABLE VIEW, I prefer to just go to the DATA VIEW and adjust the columns manually. Since all 6 columns are clearly visible, there is nothing you need to do, but if you had a lot of columns, you could make them smaller, or increase them to fit some of the larger values entered. Just click between the variable names and use the arrow to adjust accordingly. When you are finished with this initial setup of the imported file, it is time to save it.

Go to FILE → SAVE AS and enter the file name. For this example, I used <u>GRADES.sav</u>. Then click SAVE.

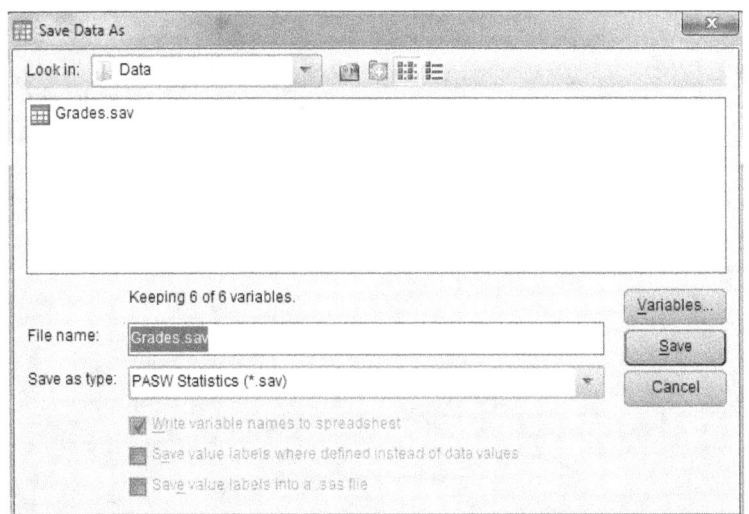

CHAPTER 3: RECODING DATA

Once you have your raw data loaded into SPSS, you can then begin to apply formulas and manipulate the data to suit you. Let's look at the <u>GRADES.sav</u> file to see what we can do.

	Name	Profile	Track	Exam	Term_Paper	Participation
1	Abby	1	3	38	48	10
2	Bob	0	2	40	45	9
3	Chloe	1	1	32	40	8
4	David	1	2	35	50	9
5	Ellie	0	1	36	35	7
6	Frank	1	1	24	30	8
7	Gretchen	1	3	28	42	10
8	Hank	0	2	40	49	7
9	Irene	1	1	33	38	9
10	Justin	1	1	36	40	10

Let's supposed we wanted a column to show the learner's total points for the course. We need to create a formula for this.

Go to TRANSFORM →
COMPUTE VARIABLE.

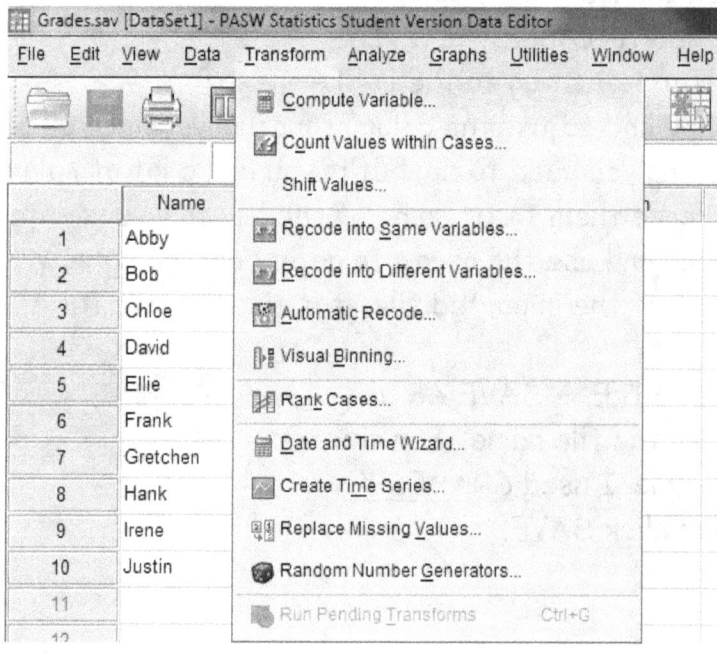

You will see this display. We need to create a variable <u>Total</u> and enter a formula using the variables already in the file.

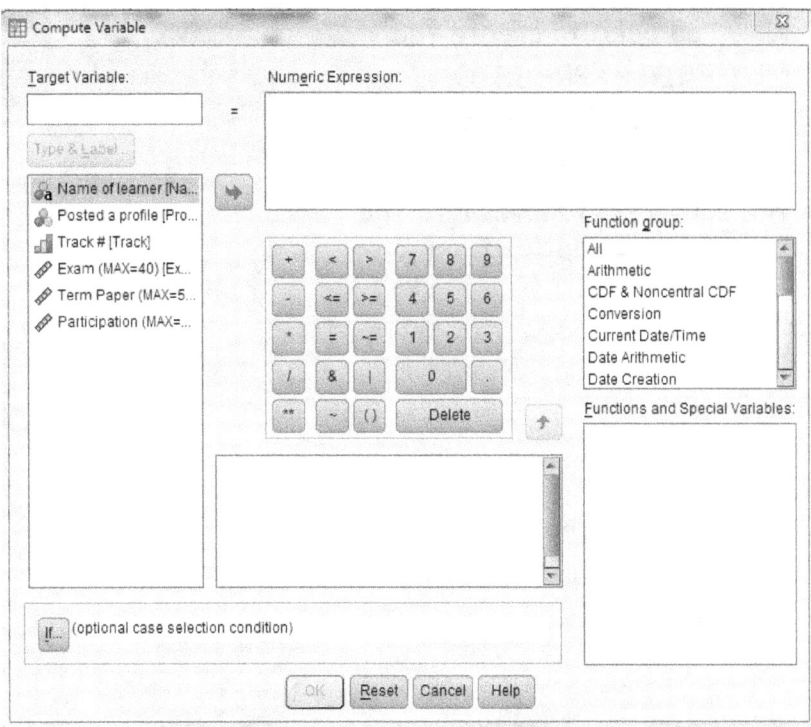

Enter <u>Total</u> as the TARGET VARIABLE. Then click on TYPE & LABEL. Enter "Course Total" as the LABEL and then CONTINUE.

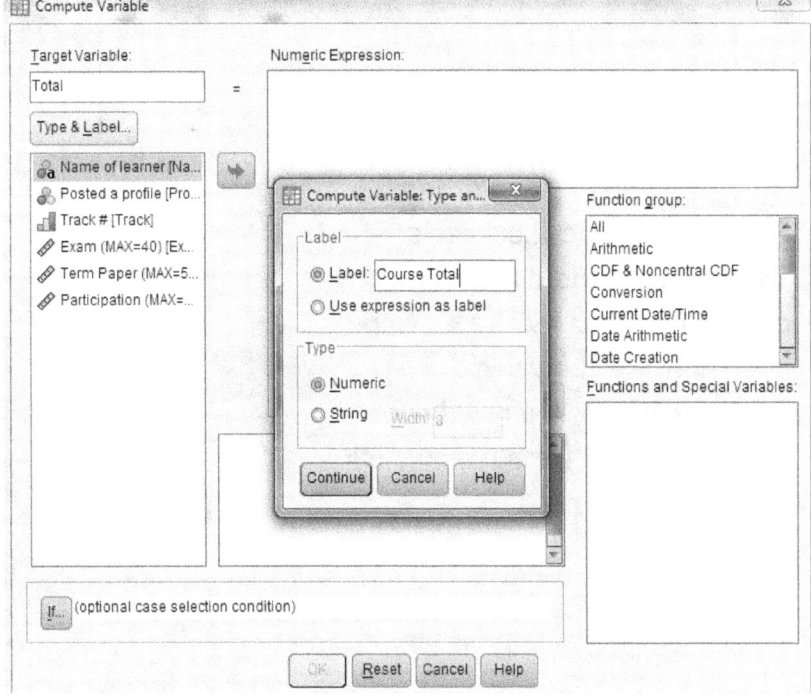

Now you need to create the NUMERIC EXPRESSION. Select <u>Exam</u> (shown as "Exam (MAX=40) [Exam]") and click on the arrow so it moves into the NUMERIC EXPRESSION box.

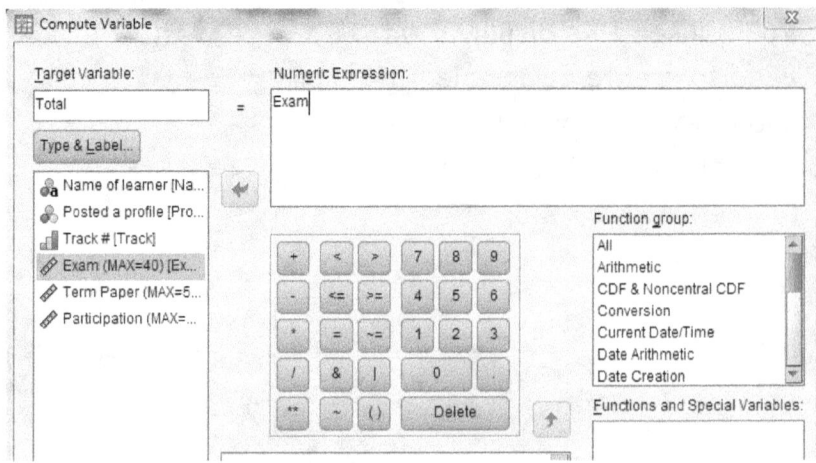

Then click on the + symbol so you can continue to add to the formula.

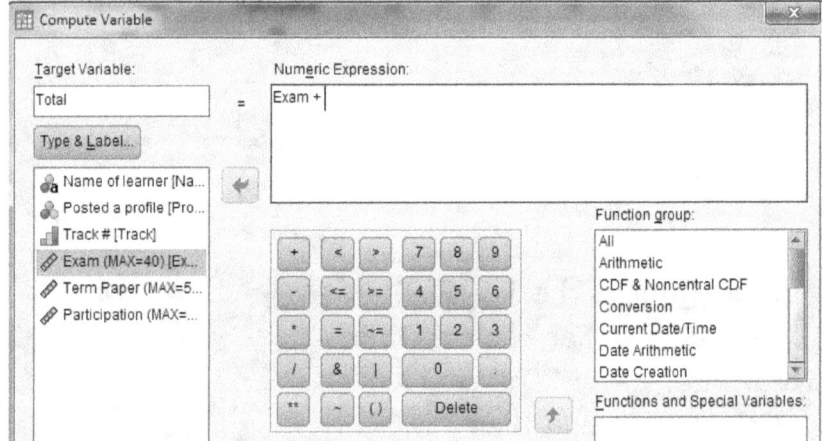

Next select the "Learner's Term Paper" and click on the arrow, followed by the + symbol and then the "Learner's Participation." You now have the completed formula, so click OK.

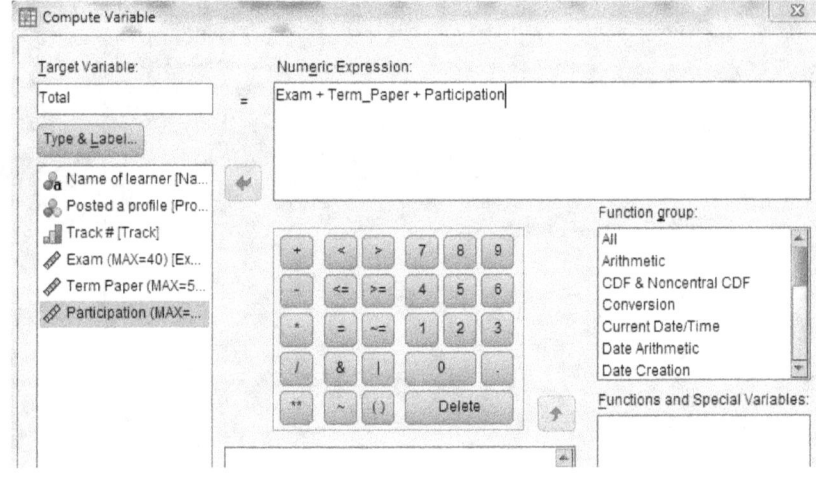

	Name	Profile	Track	Exam	Term_Paper	Participation	Total
1	Abby	1	3	38	48	10	96
2	Bob	0	2	40	45	9	94
3	Chloe	1	1	32	40	8	80
4	David	1	2	35	50	9	94
5	Ellie	0	1	36	35	7	78
6	Frank	1	1	24	30	8	62
7	Gretchen	1	3	28	42	10	80
8	Hank	0	2	40	49	7	96
9	Irene	1	1	33	38	9	80
10	Justin	1	1	36	40	10	86

You now see a new column <u>Total</u> which consists of the sum of the three scores to the left of it.   The variable was set up with 2 decimal values, so you can choose to go to VARIABLE VIEW and change the number of DECIMALS if you wish. Go ahead and do it for practice (shown below).

	Name	Type	Width	Decimals	Label	Values	Missing	Columns	Align	Measure	Role
1	Name	String	8	0	Name of learner	None	None	8	Left	Nominal	Input
2	Profile	Numeric	1	0	Posted a profile	{0, NO}...	None	11	Center	Nominal	Input
3	Track	Numeric	1	0	Track #	None	None	11	Center	Ordinal	Input
4	Exam	Numeric	2	0	Exam (MAX=40)	None	None	11	Center	Scale	Input
5	Term_Paper	Numeric	2	0	Term Paper (MAX=50)	None	None	13	Center	Scale	Input
6	Participation	Numeric	2	0	Participation (MAX=10)	None	None	13	Center	Scale	Input
7	Total	Numeric	2	0	Course Total	None	None	10	Center	Scale	Input

	Name	Profile	Track	Exam	Term_Paper	Participation	Total
1	Abby	1	3	38	48	10	96
2	Bob	0	2	40	45	9	94
3	Chloe	1	1	32	40	8	80
4	David	1	2	35	50	9	94
5	Ellie	0	1	36	35	7	78
6	Frank	1	0	24	30	8	62
7	Gretchen	1	3	28	42	10	80
8	Hank	0	2	40	49	7	96
9	Irene	1	1	33	38	9	80
10	Justin	1	1	36	40	10	86

Now we need to set up a column whereby we assign course grades based on the <u>Total</u>. Go to TRANSFORM → RECODE INTO DIFFERENT VARIABLES.

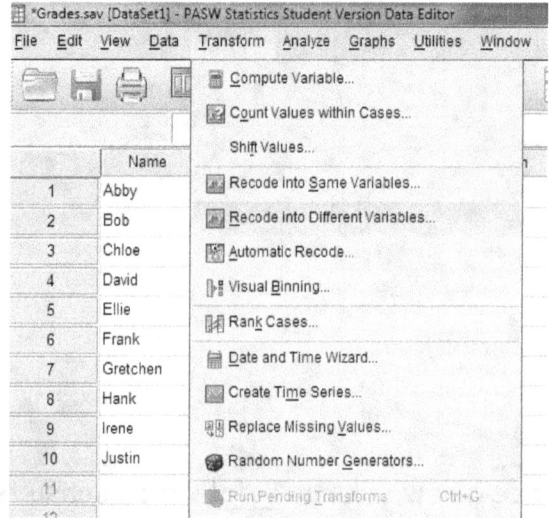

Choose <u>Total</u> and click on the arrow since that is the INPUT VARIABLE by which the "Course Grade" is to be determined.

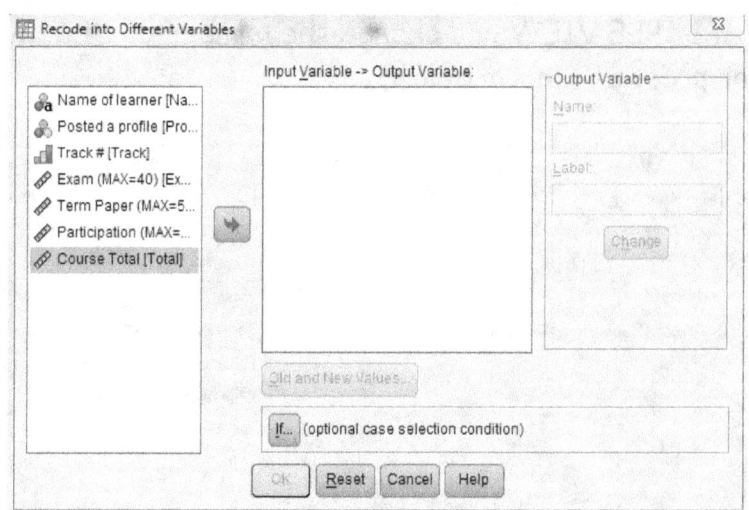

Now you need to enter the OUTPUT VARIABLE. Let's use <u>Grade</u> with a LABEL of "Course Grade". Then click CHANGE.

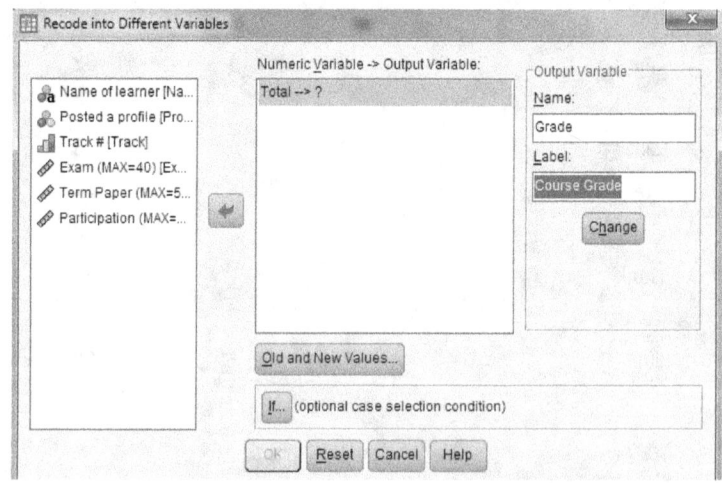

You should see the big box showing TOTAL → GRADE since the <u>Total</u> is being used to determine the <u>Grade</u>. Now click on OLD AND NEW VALUES.

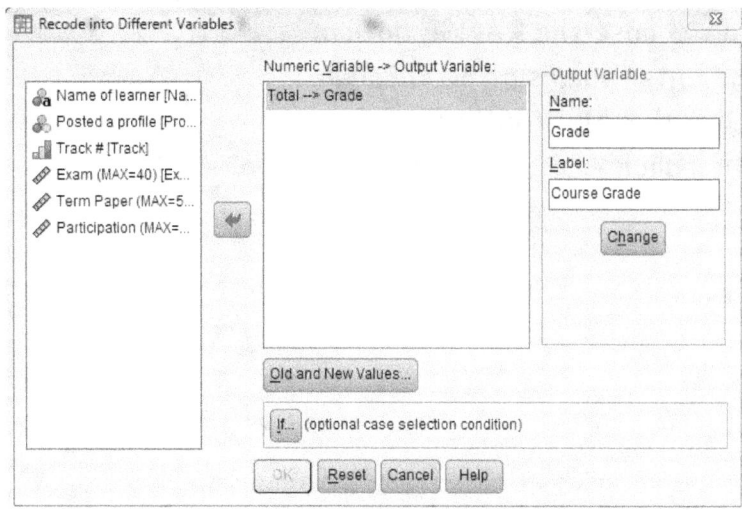

Since we are using the conventional grading system, let's start with the top grade. Choose the RANGE, VALUE THROUGH HIGHEST and enter 90 in the box. Since this is not numeric, check the box OUTPUT VARIABLES ARE STRINGS and enter a WIDTH of 1 since letter grades only require one character. Then enter a NEW VALUE of A. Then click ADD.

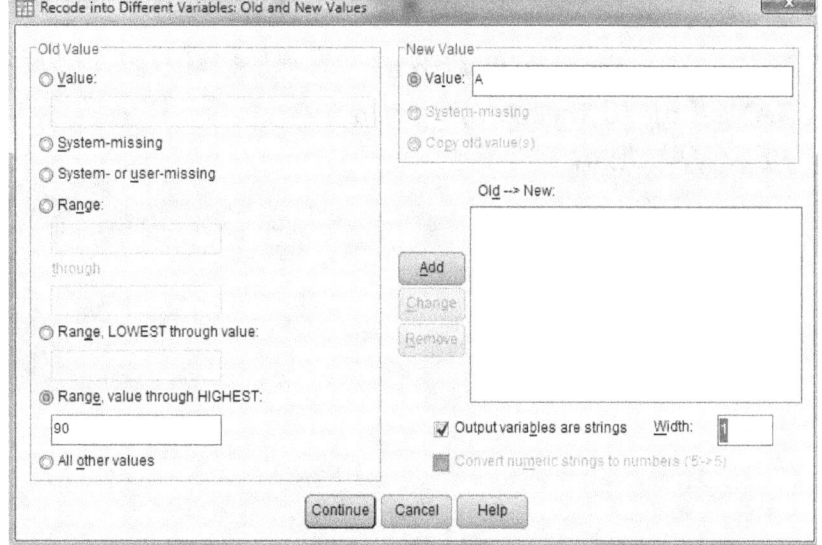

You now see the OLD→NEW box displays the first rule in which an A is determined by a grade of 90 and above. Now let's add the rest.

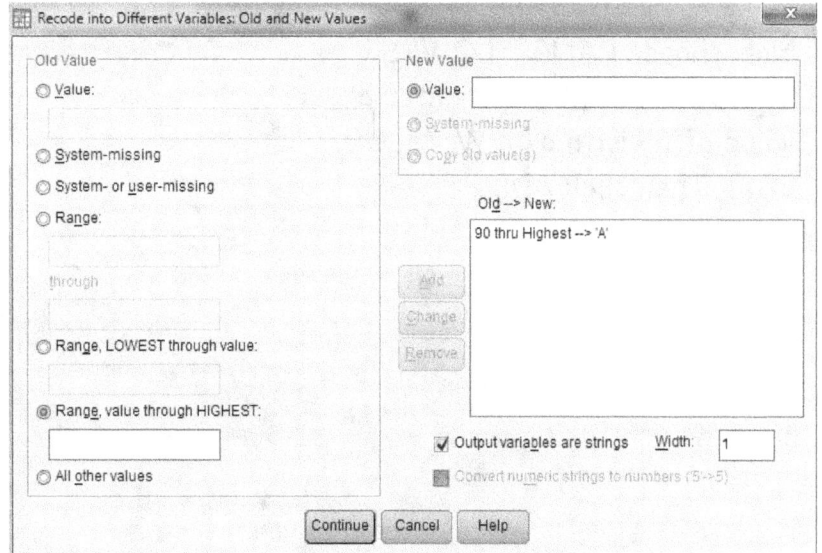

Now choose the RANGE option and enter values of 80 through 89, with a NEW VALUE of B. Then click ADD.

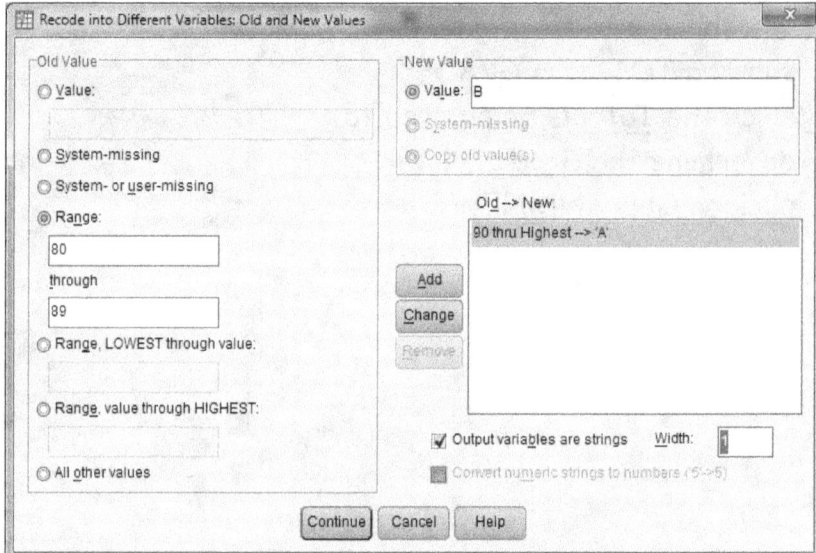

Repeat the procedure with a RANGE of 70 through 79 for a NEW VALUE of C.

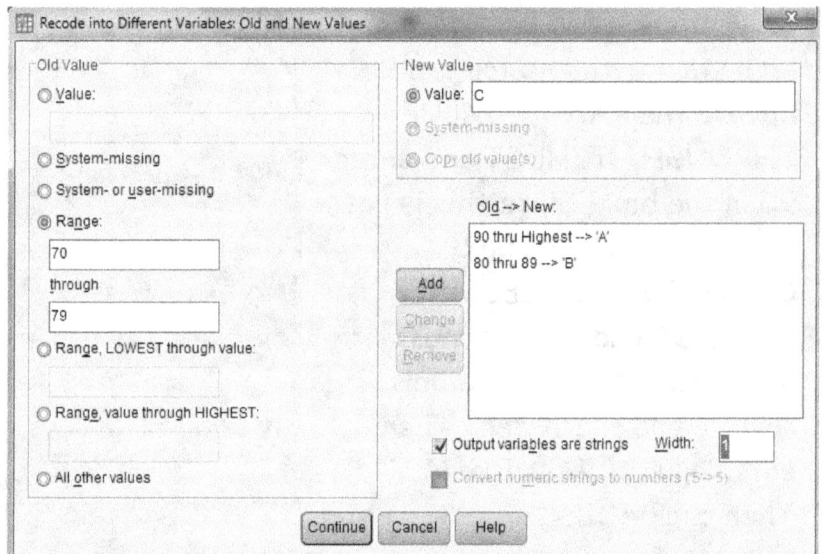

Now choose RANGE, LOWEST THROUGH VALUE and enter a value of 69 with a NEW VALUE of F. Then click ADD.

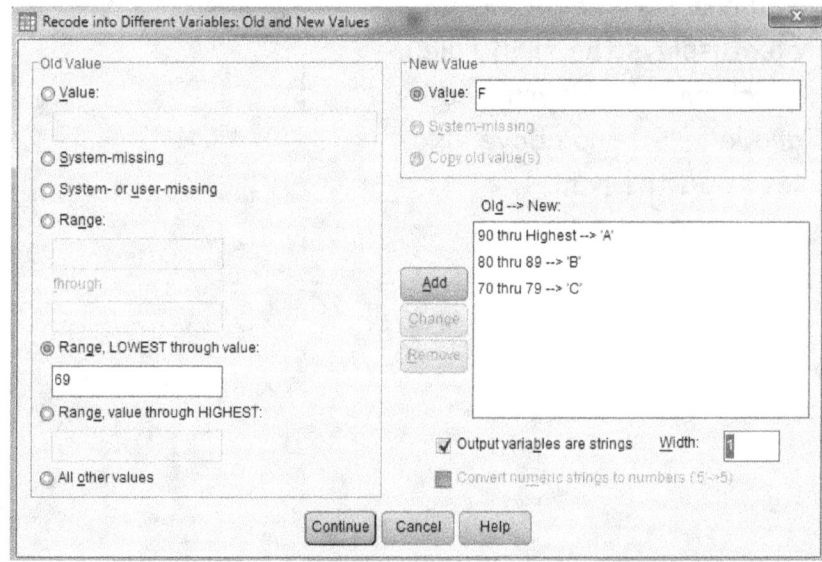

Now all of the rules are set, so click on CONTINUE and OK.

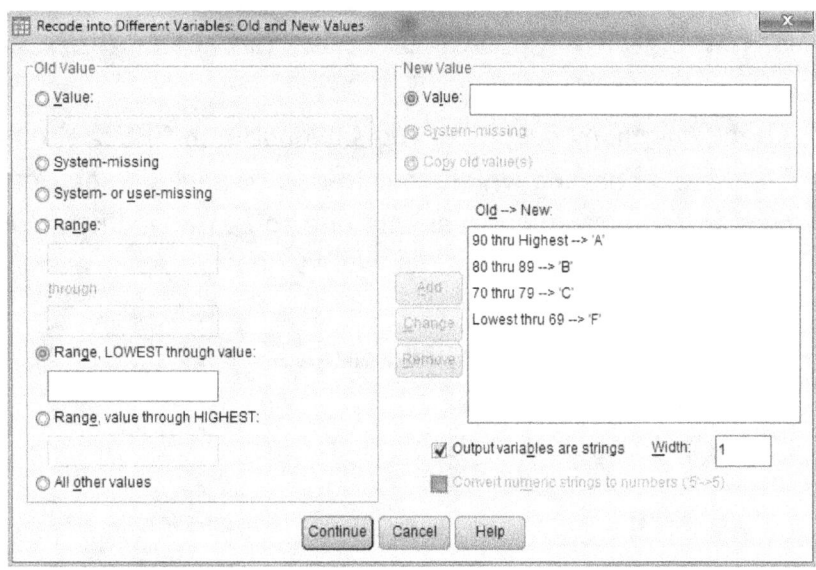

	Name	Profile	Track	Exam	Term_Paper	Participation	Total	Grade
1	Abby	1	3	38	48	10	96	A
2	Bob	0	2	40	45	9	94	A
3	Chloe	1	1	32	40	8	80	B
4	David	1	2	35	50	9	94	A
5	Ellie	0	1	36	35	7	78	C
6	Frank	1	1	24	30	8	62	F
7	Gretchen	1	3	28	42	10	80	B
8	Hank	0	2	40	49	7	96	A
9	Irene	1	1	33	38	9	80	B
10	Justin	1	1	36	40	10	86	B

You now see a new column <u>Grade</u> with the appropriate letter grade entered. Feel free to CENTER the column if you wish.

Save the file again.

You have now experienced some of the most common procedures used in setting up SPSS data files.

CHAPTER 4: DESCRIPTIVE STATISTICS & GRAPHICAL ANALYSIS

There are many graphical tools available in SPSS. You can see the lengthy menu under GRAPHS. Knowing which tool to use requires some basic statistical knowledge, so for now, let's just try out a simple one to get acquainted with the features.

Let's stick with the GRADES.sav file. To make a pie chart, go to GRAPHS → LEGACY DIALOGS → PIE.

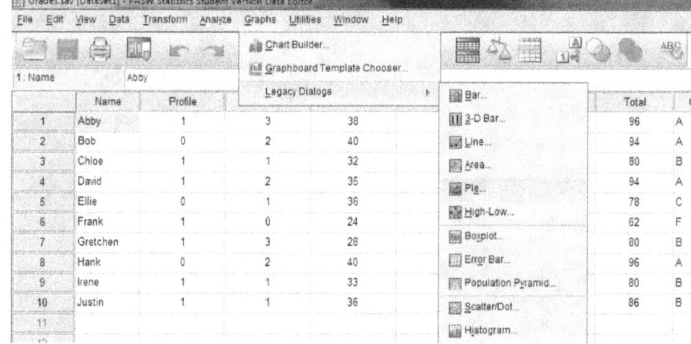

Leave the default alone on the pop-up window and click DEFINE.

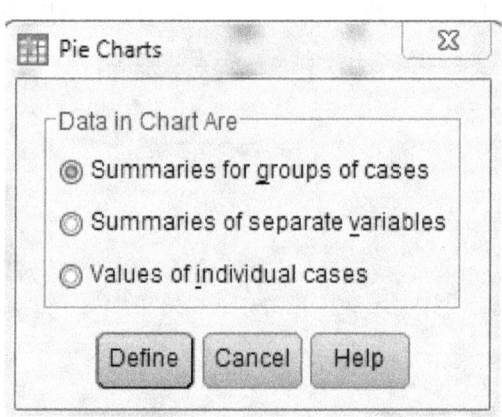

Now click on <u>Grade</u> and click on the arrow for the DEFINE SLICES BY box.

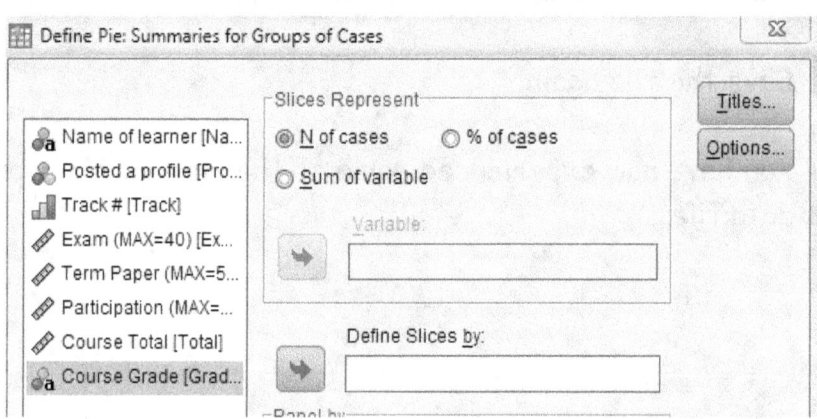

You can opt to display the pie with actual totals in each slice or percentages. For now, choose % OF CASES. Then click OK.

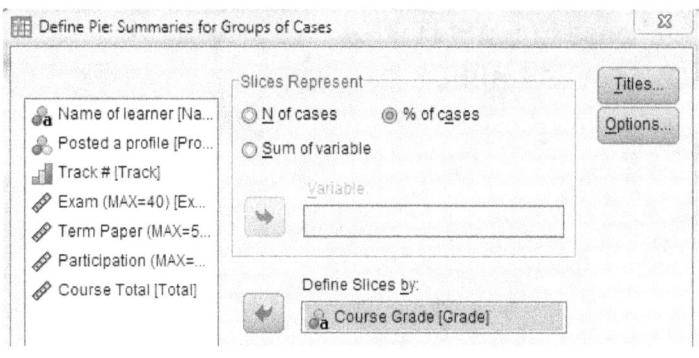

Here you see the output generated. There is a menu on the left that allows you to navigate the output, which helps when the output file gets lengthy.

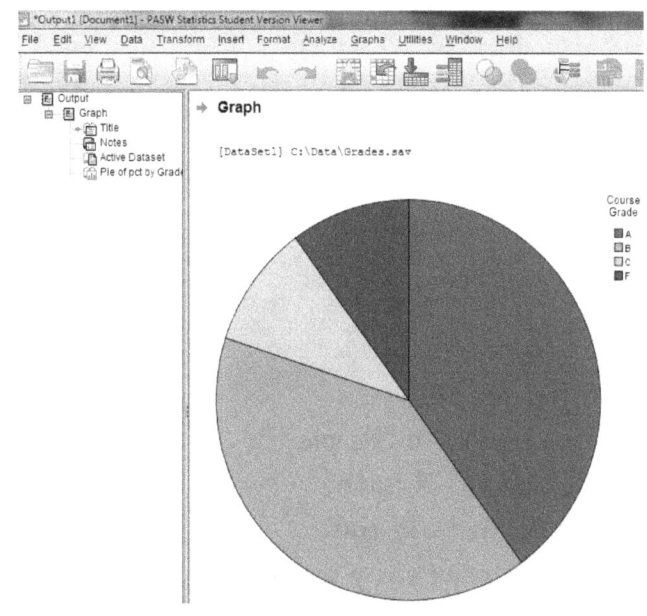

If you want to add labels to the graph, double click on the Pie Chart and it will take you to the Chart Editor.

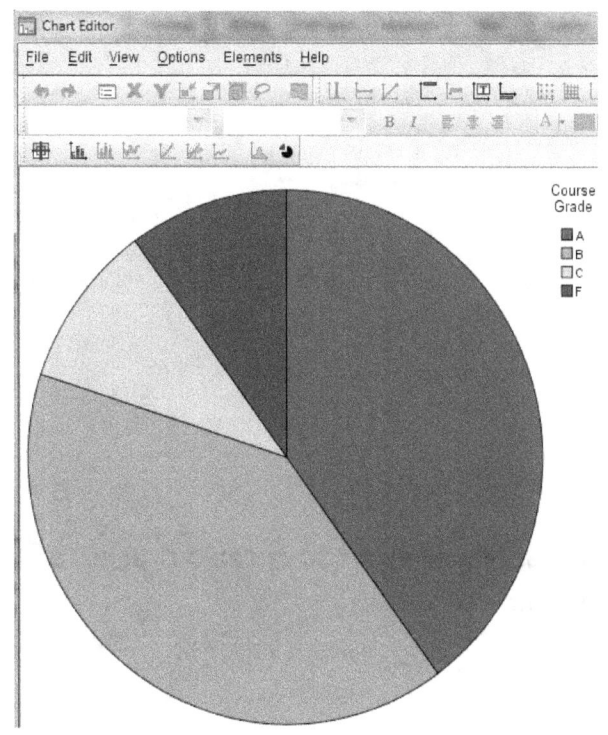

Now choose ELEMENTS →
SHOW DATA LABELS

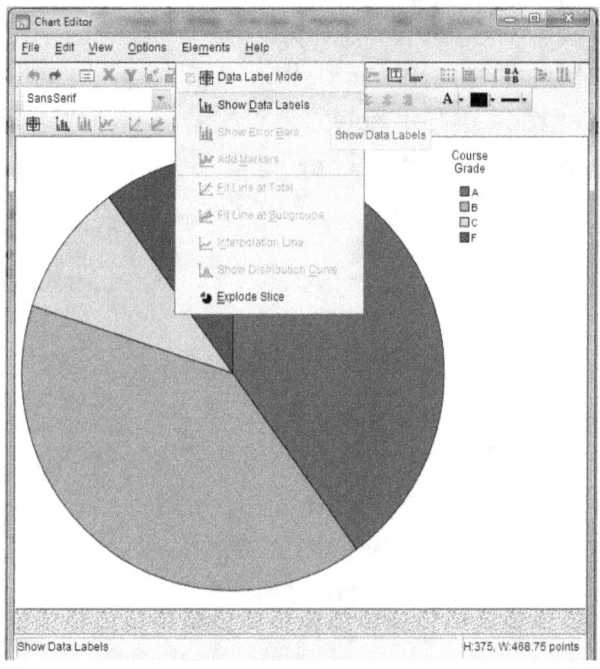

And here you see the
percentages added to the pie
slices. Click on the X in the
upper right corner and the
graph will be permanently saved
to the output.

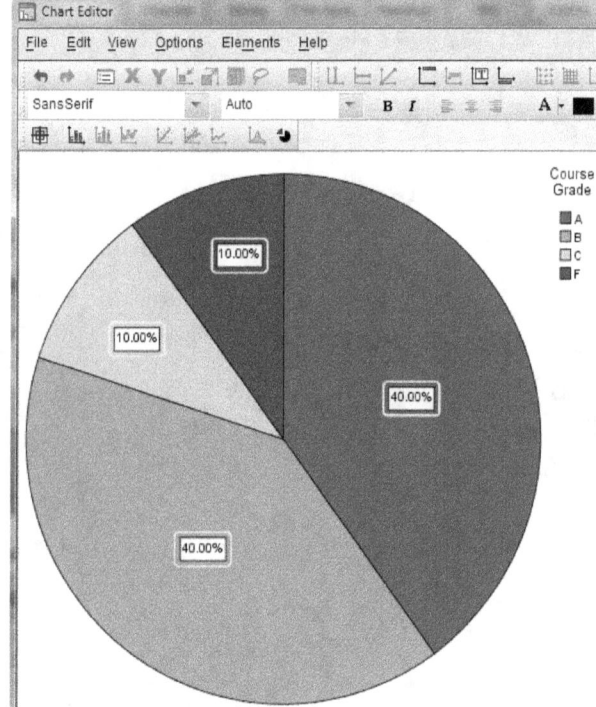

Now suppose you wanted to filter out some of the data first before conducting analysis,
for whatever reason.

Go to DATA → SELECT CASES.

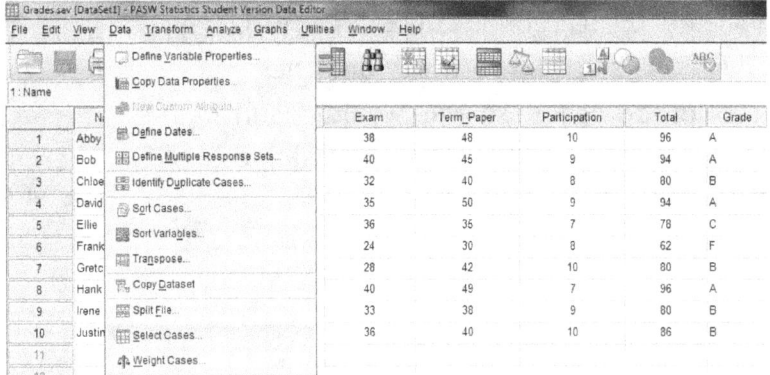

Now choose IF CONDITION IS SATISFIED and click on the IF button.

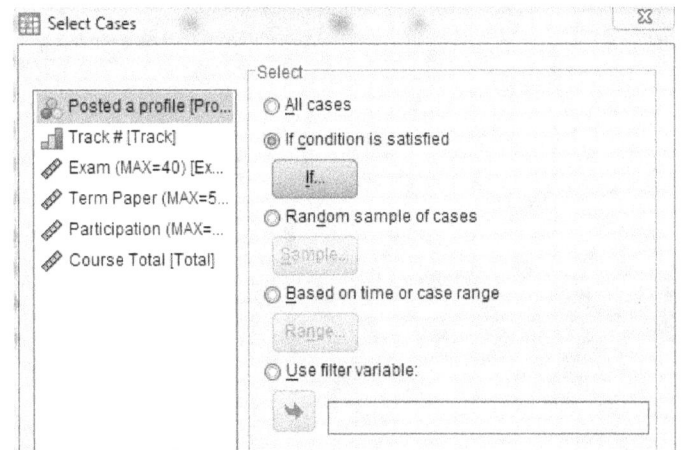

If we wanted to only look at learners who were not track 3, then we should select <u>Track</u> and then click on the arrow. Then select the ~= symbol to indicate "not equals" followed by a 3.

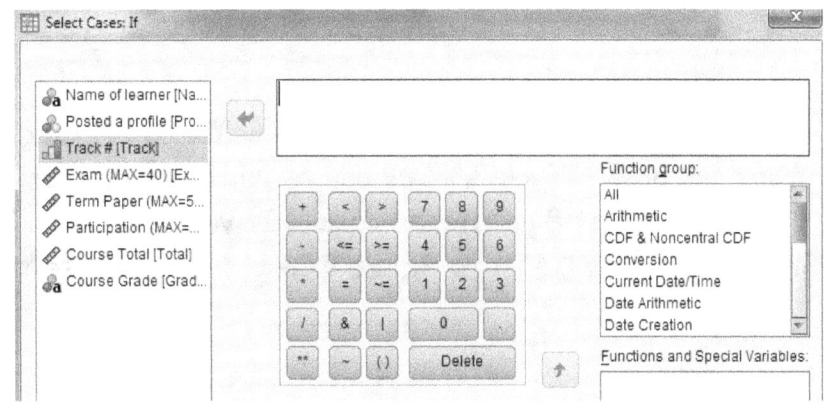

This is how the function should look. You could have done this as "Track < 3" if you preferred. Click CONTINUE.

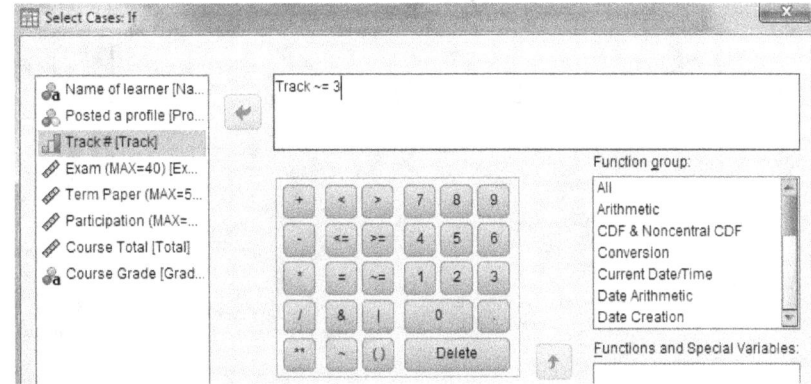

You see the IF condition as directed. The OUTPUT is set up to filter out the unselected cases, so this would result in eliminating those learners in "Track 3." Click OK.

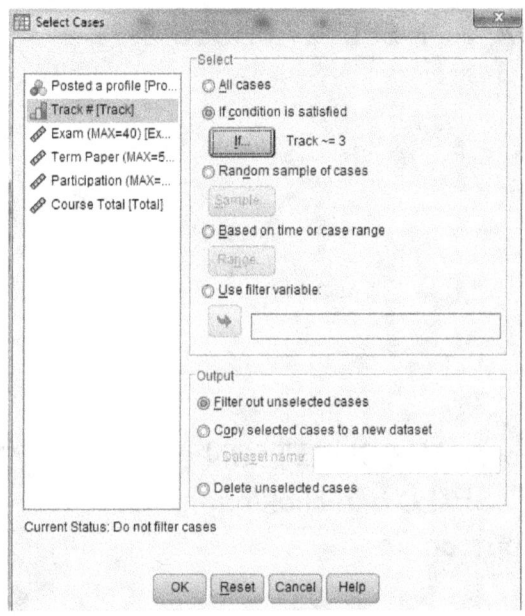

	Name	Profile	Track	Exam	Term_Paper	Participation	Total	Grade	filter_$
1	Abby	1	3	38	48	10	96	A	0
2	Bob	0	2	40	45	9	94	A	1
3	Chloe	1	1	32	40	8	80	B	1
4	David	1	2	35	50	9	94	A	1
5	Ellie	0	1	36	35	7	78	C	1
6	Frank	1	1	24	30	8	62	F	1
7	Gretchen	1	3	28	42	10	80	B	0
8	Hank	0	2	40	49	7	96	A	1
9	Irene	1	1	33	38	9	80	B	1
10	Justin	1	1	36	40	10	86	B	1

Now if you look at the data, you will see a slash through Abby's and Gretchen's rows, as they are both "Track 3." You can re-run the PIE chart or any other graph, and it will only be based on the 8 unfiltered cases. If you want to go back to using all of the data, you need only go to DATA → SELECT CASES and choose the ALL CASES option.

Let's try out a BAR graph.

Go to GRAPHS → LEGACY DIALOGS →BAR.

Choose SIMPLE and DEFINE.

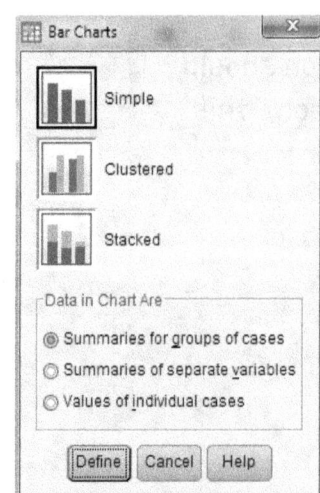

Choose <u>Grade</u> for the CATEGORY AXIS and choose N OF CASES (which shows the actual sample size). Then OK.

The output shows only 8 students as expected.

If you would like to enhance the chart, you may do so via the CHART EDITOR by double-clicking on the bar chart, but let's move on.

→ **Graph**

[DataSet1] C:\Data\Grades.sav

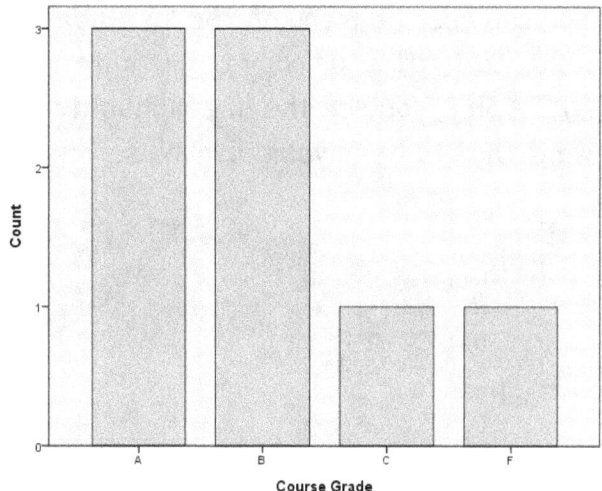

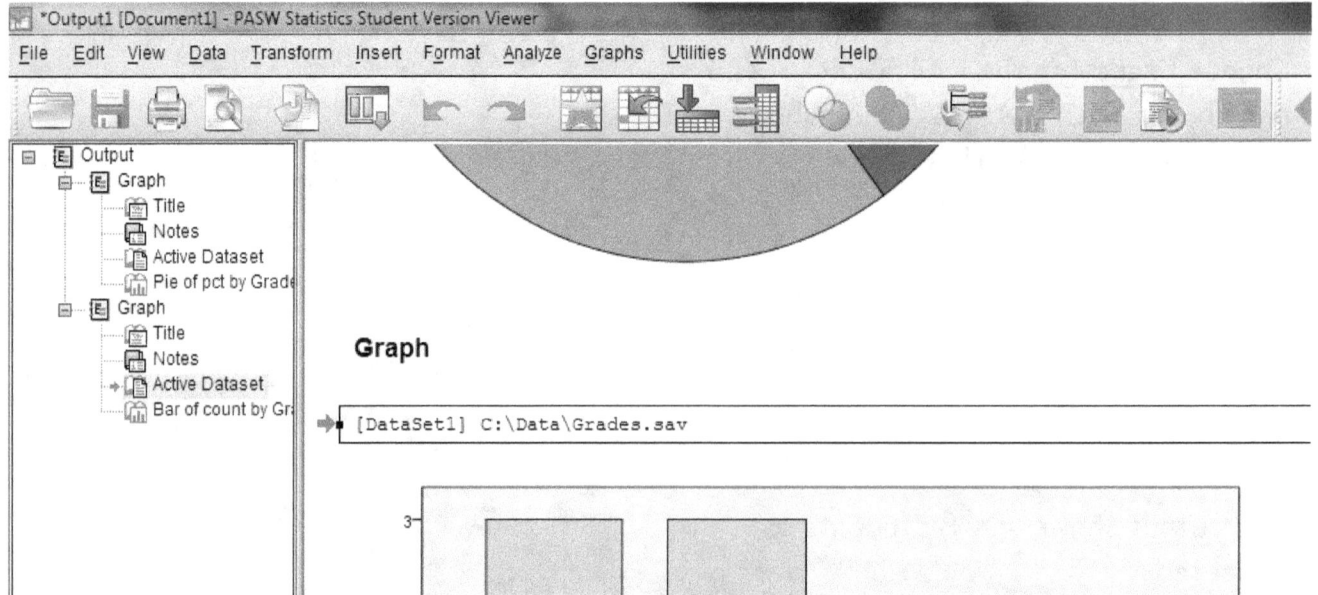

You can see the menu on the left side of the output growing. You can delete what you want, edit titles, or copy output into Word. Let's try a few. If you click on ACTIVE DATASET, you see the line highlighted which shows the data file name. You may not want that to be in your display, so you can right-click the item and CUT.

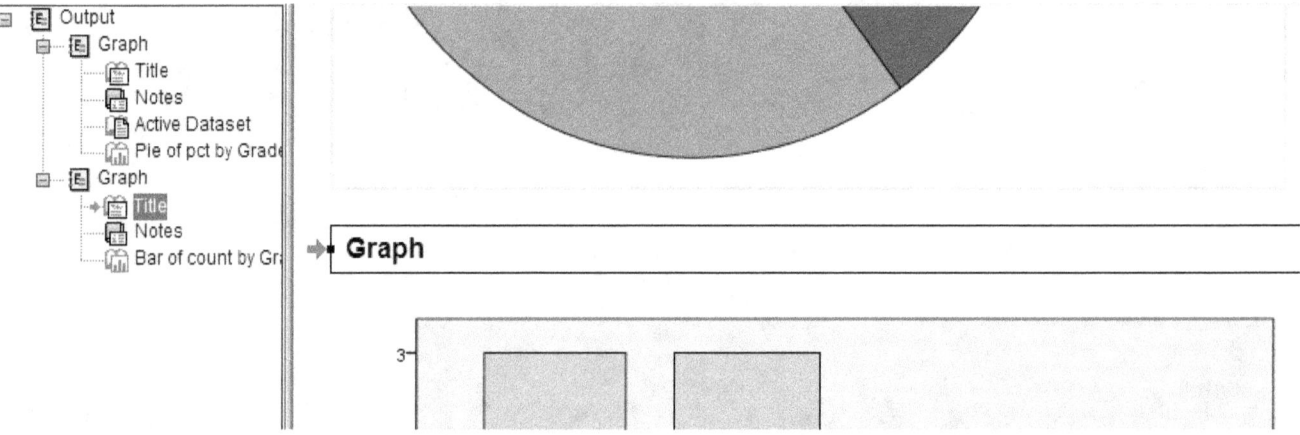

Suppose you wanted to have a more descriptive title. Click on TITLE and then double-click on the word GRAPH so you can change the label accordingly.

Edit the TITLE as you wish. Here I not only changed the wording but also changed the font to Comic Sans.

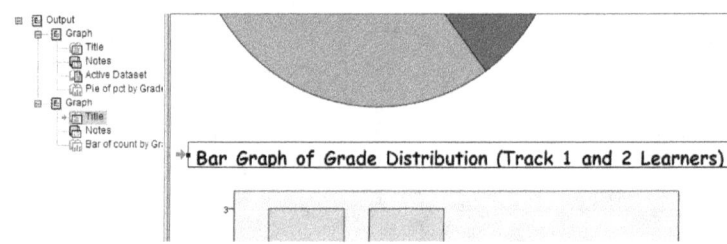

Before proceeding, save this output file. This is good common practice.

Go to FILE → SAVE AS and name the file as you wish, then click SAVE. For this example, I used GRADES.spv.

The output file will automatically have an SPV extension (it was SPO in older versions of SPSS).

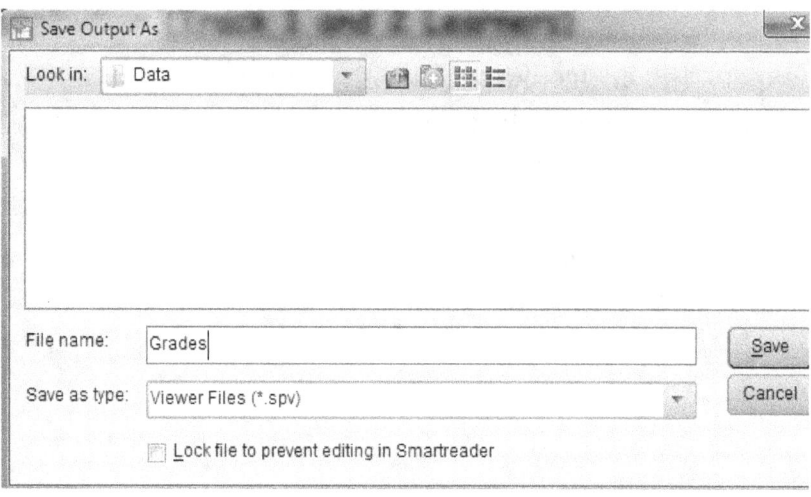

Now suppose you wanted to copy select portions of the output into a Word document.

Go to the menu on the left of the output, choose what you want to copy, then right-click and choose COPY. You could also directly click on the graph and right-click and choose COPY. You may click on several items at once and also right-click and COPY. Or you may also wish to use the EXPORT option instead which directly puts your chosen objects into an Excel, Word or HTML file.

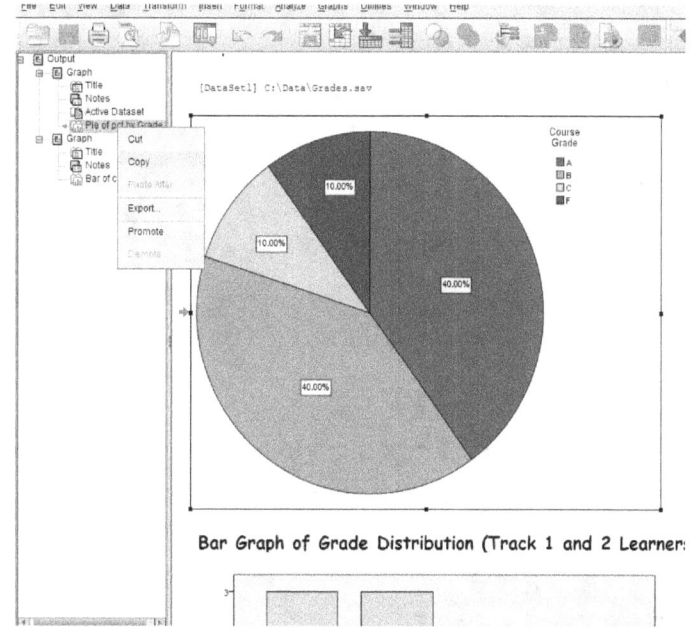

Next, if you chose to COPY, then go into MS Word and choose PASTE. The pie chart will appear in the Word document. When you create your analysis chapter of your dissertation, you will need to incorporate output, so this will prove helpful.

If you wish, you could actually export the entire output file at once and then delete what you don't want when you get to Word. Just go to FILE → EXPORT and choose the name, file type and location.

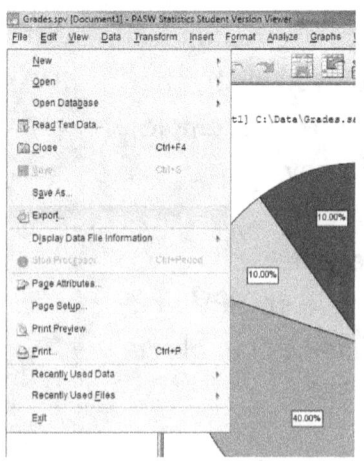

Before proceeding with some of the analytical tools, let's go back to using all of the data.

Go to DATA → SELECT CASES and choose the ALL CASES option.

Then click OK.

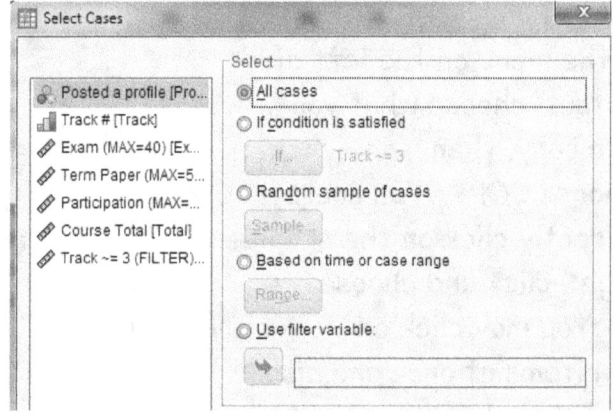

The ANALYZE menu has many great statistical tools ranging from simple descriptive statistics to advanced inferential statistics. Let's try a couple of them.

Go to ANALYZE → DESCRIPTIVE STATISTICS → FREQUENCIES

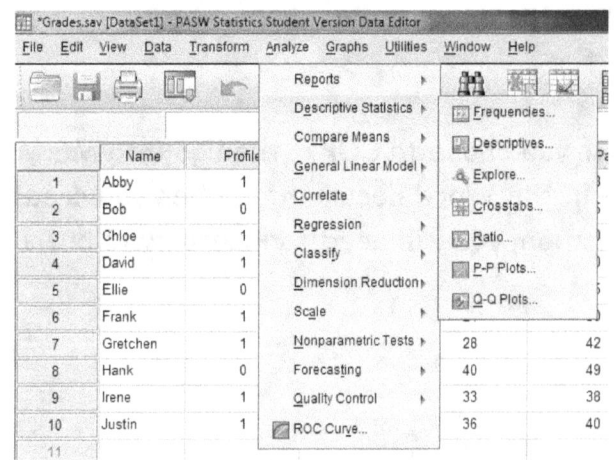

Here you can select as many variables as you wish. Since Frequencies are only appropriate where there is repetition, choose <u>Profile</u>, <u>Track</u>, <u>Total</u> and <u>Grade</u>. Click on the arrow to move those variables to the empty box (one at a time or all at once doesn't matter).

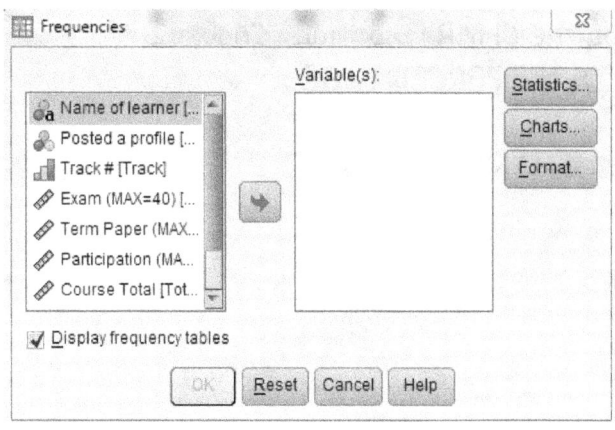

Make sure the DISPLAY FREQUENCY TABLES box is checked.

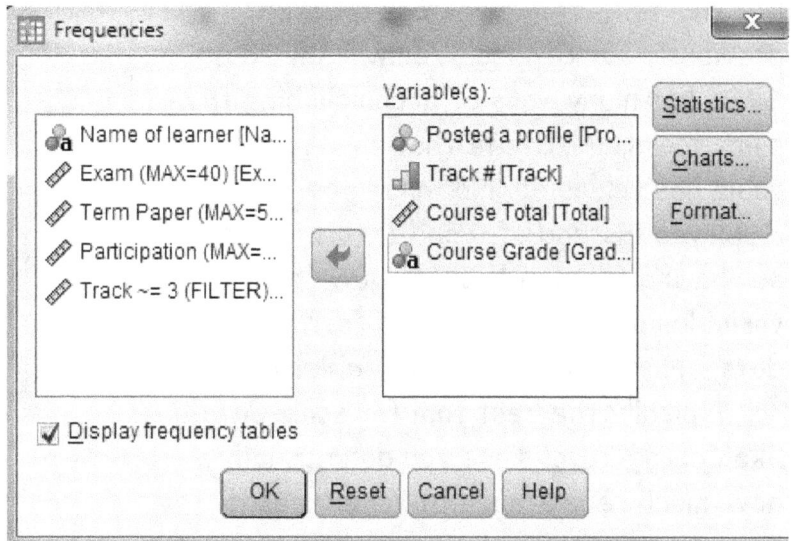

Click on the STATISTICS option. These options are really only appropriate for Scale data like TOTAL. Even though it is nonsense to compute a mean for the other nominal variables, SPSS will still do it because it sees numbers. But we can delete what we don't need later. Click on CONTINUE.

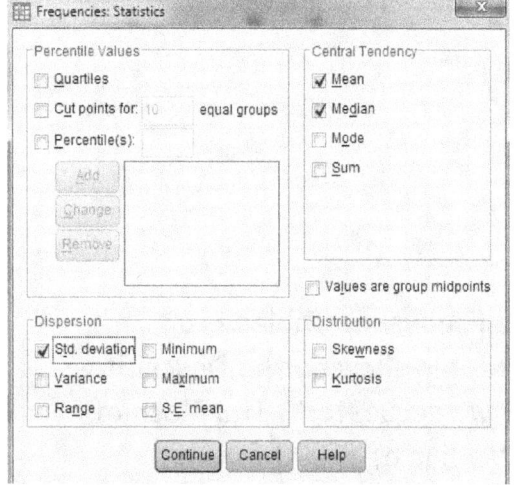

Click on the CHARTS option. Choose BAR CHARTS and PERCENTAGES.

Then CONTINUE and OK.

We generated 4 frequency tables for the chosen variables. We also generated 4 bar charts, just like the one created previously for <u>Grades</u>. You will see that SPSS has many ways of accomplishing the same tasks. Also note that the <u>Profile</u> table has values of "No" and "Yes" displayed instead of 0 and 1; this is due to our having filled in the VALUES for these variables so as to substitute for the raw data. Note that Frequency tables are not typically the best tool for scale data, like <u>Course Total</u> since you don't usually have much repetition, but sometimes it helps to see what you have and then delete what doesn't work well.

Course Total

		Frequency	Percent	Valid Percent	Cumulative Percent
Valid	62	1	10.0	10.0	10.0
	78	1	10.0	10.0	20.0
	80	3	30.0	30.0	50.0
	86	1	10.0	10.0	60.0
	94	2	20.0	20.0	80.0
	96	2	20.0	20.0	100.0
	Total	10	100.0	100.0	

Course Grade

		Frequency	Percent	Valid Percent	Cumulative Percent
Valid	A	4	40.0	40.0	40.0
	B	4	40.0	40.0	80.0
	C	1	10.0	10.0	90.0
	F	1	10.0	10.0	100.0
	Total	10	100.0	100.0	

Bar Chart

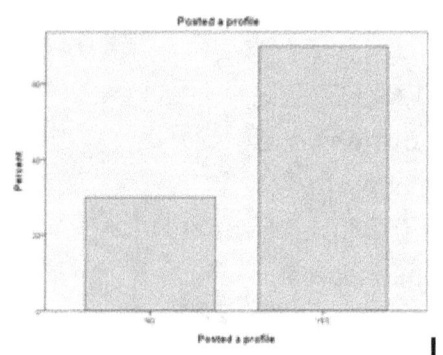

Above the Frequency Tables is a Statistics table showing the Descriptive Statistics we requested. The Mean of 84.6 and Median of 83.00 for the <u>Course Total</u> is useful, but the Mean <u>Profile</u> response of .70 makes no sense.

Statistics		Posted a profile	Track #	Course Total	Course Grade
N	Valid	10	10	10	10
	Missing	0	0	0	0
Mean		.70	1.70	84.60	
Median		1.00	1.50	83.00	
Std. Deviation		.483	.823	10.834	

If you really want the Statistics for just <u>Course Total</u> (and maybe the other grades), just rerun this option for just those variables and delete this table. SPSS often involves experimentation to see what you get.

You will find that there are many ways to get to the same type of information in SPSS. Descriptive Statistics is often an option on other menus, as are several types of graphs, but the different menus sometimes vary in what they offer (e.g., sometimes you get only a few Descriptive Statistics to choose from and sometimes you get all of them). Had you gone to ANALYZE → DESCRIPTIVE STATISTICS → DESCRIPTIVES, you would see an identical menu and resulting output as compared to the statistics you got from FREQUENCIES. But let's look at a different one that offers special features (and is the one I actually use first for conducting analysis.

Go to ANALYZE → DESCRIPTIVE STATISTICS → EXPLORE.

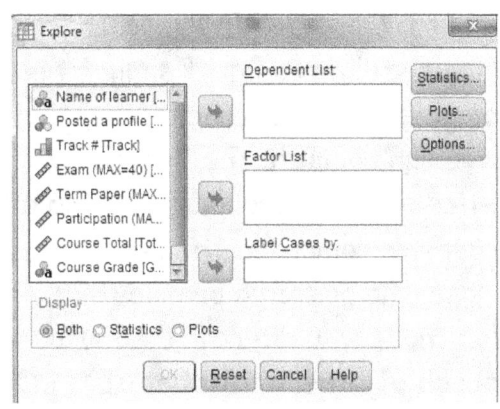

Choose <u>Total</u> for the Dependent List and <u>Profile</u> for the Factor List. This will analyze the "Course Totals" for those who posted a profile vs. those who did not. In the DISPLAY section, choose the STATISTICS option (since we don't need graphs here). Then click on the STATISTICS button.

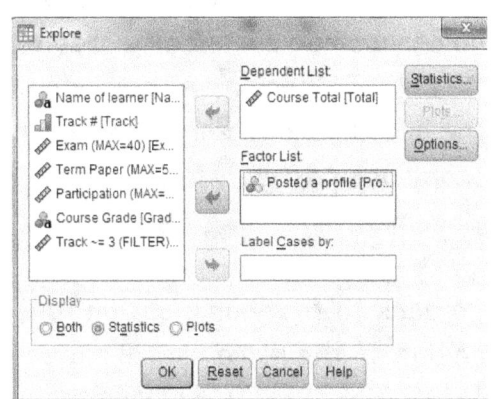

Check the DESCRIPTIVES box to get the basic descriptive statistics. Then CONTINUE and OK.

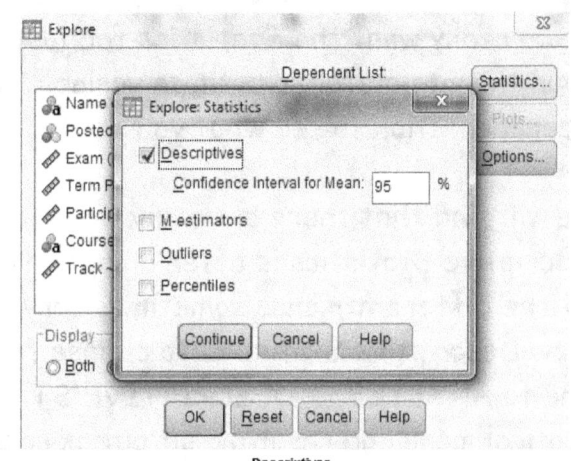

In the output you will see some common statistics computed. Notice what you get from this EXPLORE option, which is a bit different from the FREQUENCIES option but still has a lot of similarities. The biggest difference here, though, is that you can compute the descriptive statistics for a subgroup of a variable (in this case, we computed the average grade for those who posted a profile (82.57) and for those who did not (89.33), as well as a bunch of other statistics. EXPLORE lets you dig into layers within variables, and you can also do some basic graphs too using the PLOTS option on that menu. As with the graphs shown earlier, you can easily copy and paste this output into a word document.

Descriptives

	Posted a profile			Statistic	Std. Error
Course Total	NO	Mean		89.33	5.696
		95% Confidence Interval for Mean	Lower Bound	64.83	
			Upper Bound	113.84	
		5% Trimmed Mean		.	
		Median		94.00	
		Variance		97.333	
		Std. Deviation		9.866	
		Minimum		78	
		Maximum		96	
		Range		18	
		Interquartile Range		.	
		Skewness		-1.652	1.225
		Kurtosis		.	
	YES	Mean		82.57	4.270
		95% Confidence Interval for Mean	Lower Bound	72.12	
			Upper Bound	93.02	
		5% Trimmed Mean		82.97	
		Median		80.00	
		Variance		127.619	
		Std. Deviation		11.297	
		Minimum		62	
		Maximum		96	
		Range		34	
		Interquartile Range		14	
		Skewness		-.777	.794
		Kurtosis		1.160	1.587

Let's go back to that same option to explore one of the more useful plots. Go to ANALYZE → DESCRIPTIVE STATISTICS → EXPLORE, choose <u>Total</u> for the Dependent List but this time leave the Factor List blank (you could have subgroups, but I want you to see this tool as single group for now). Make sure that PLOTS is marked in the DISPLAY area. Now click on the PLOTS button.

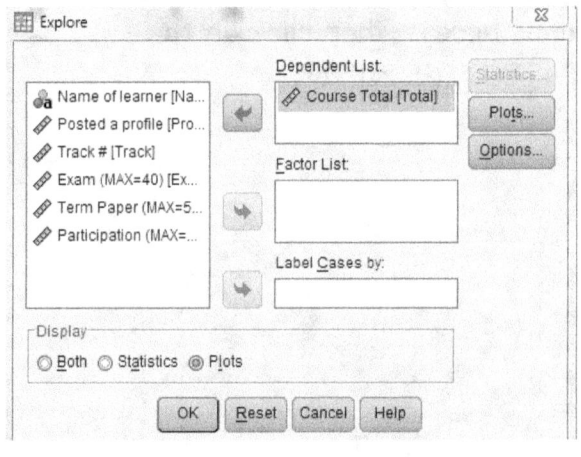

Let's keep the defaults in place. We wish to see the STEM-AND-LEAF plot and the BOXPLOT (we have already seen the HISTOGRAM). CONTINUE and OK.

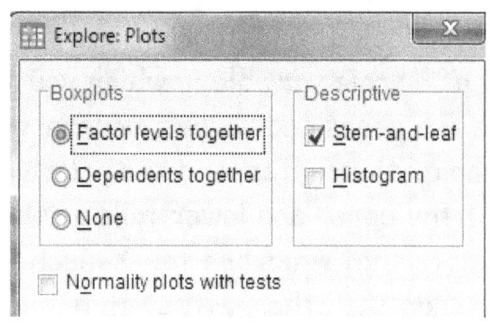

The BOXPLOT shows the spread of the data while telling you some of the descriptive statistics.   The middle line in each box is the MEDIAN which tells us that exactly half of the data is above and half below that value. The top of each box is the UPPER QUARTILE or 75th PERCENTILE which tells us that 75% of the data is below that value, so only 25%

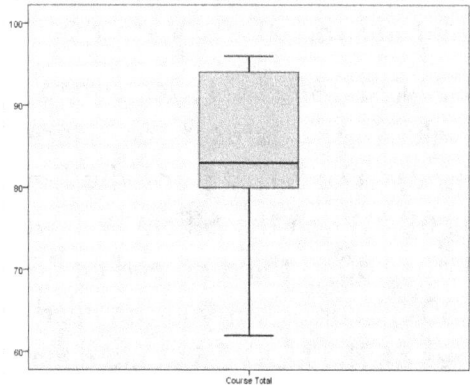

are above it. The bottom of each box is the LOWER QUARTILE or 25th PERCENTILE which tells us that 25% of the data is below that value. Thus the box represents the middle half of the data, with one-quarter remaining above the box and one-quarter below it. The top whisker tells us the largest value (MAXIMUM) in the data set, and the bottom whisker tells us the smallest value (MINIMUM). So these five points define the entire data set graphically. The size of the box tells us the spread of the core of the data and where the center lies, while the whiskers tell us whether the data has outliers or whether the outer half of the data close to the core. The tool's usefulness is truly shown when comparing two or more box plots simultaneously (such as the one shown in chapter 7). Comparing each group can tell you how different the distributions are, and whether the values are actually shifting up or down (look at the median mainly) and whether the spread differs (look at the size of the boxes mainly and then at the overall size of the box & whiskers together). If you displayed the distribution of daily high temperatures for each month of the year at a given city, you would expect that the medians would get higher in the Summer and lower in the winter, and that during the Summer and Winter, the spreads would be tighter than in the Fall or Spring, and the box plot would display the trends so beautifully.

When you look at a histogram, you see a graph of a scale variable in which you get to see the peaks and valleys, general location of the center, and the relative size of the upper and lower tails of the data (note that when one tail is much larger than the other, we say that the data is SKEWED in that direction, a term used a lot in Statistics). With the

```
Course Total Stem-and-Leaf Plot

Frequency     Stem &  Leaf

    1.00        6 .  2
    1.00        7 .  8
    4.00        8 .  0006
    4.00        9 .  4466

Stem width:    10
Each leaf:      1 case(s)
```

STEM-AND-LEAF PLOT, you get to still see the distribution but you can actually read every value in the dataset too. Here we see that when the STEM is 6 there is just one LEAF (a 2). The STEMS are the tens digits and the LEAVES are the ones digits, so that value is 62. When the STEM is 8, we see four LEAVES of 0006, meaning that there is an 80, another 80, a third 80 and an 86. Wow! You not only know that there are four totals in the 80-89 range but you can read them off the chart. And if you had a lot more data the sizes of the LEAVES would almost look like a histogram turned on its side with the bars removed. While a histogram can be used for any size data set, you wouldn't want to create a stem-and-leaf plot for more than 50-100 values, or you would have rows of data that just never seem to end, and its value will be negated by the chart being so busy. Note that you don't always have the stems as tens digits and the leaves as ones digits, but that is the most common design. If we were looking at body temperatures of patients in a hospital, the temperatures would likely range from 98 degrees to about 105 degrees, and the stems would represent ones digits while the leaves would represent the decimal value. So you would have a stem for 98 degrees, 99 degrees,… and the leaves of 258 might tell us that the temperatures were 99.2, 99.5 and 99.8. This is truly a great tool but only in its specific capacity.

Let's look at one more menu item that is common in conducting a basic analysis.

Go to ANALYZE → DESCRIPTIVE STATISTICS → CROSSTABS.

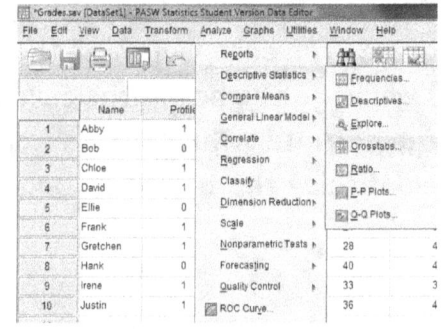

This tool is designed to count how many of the sample has specific values of 2 different variables, hence the crosstabulation. It is designed for categorical variables (nominal, sometimes ordinal, and rarely scale). Basically you don't want to have so many rows and columns that most of the counts are zeroes and ones.

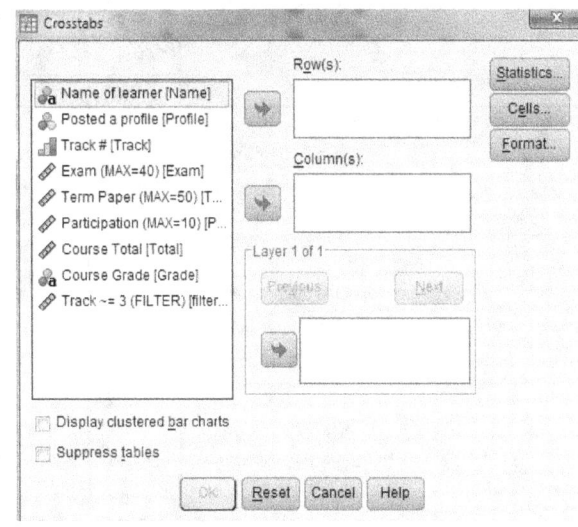

Let's put Profile in the ROWS and Course Grade in the COLUMNS, as both of these are categorical variables. Now click on STATISTICS.

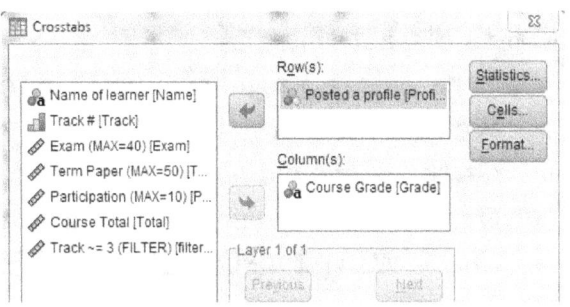

For now we don't need any of these options, but when conducting Hypothesis Testing later, these will come in handy. Click CANCEL or CONTINUE. Then click on CELLS.

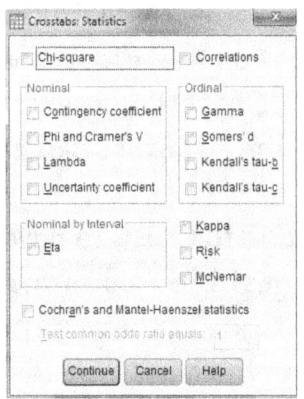

Here you want the OBSERVED box checked (which is the default). I like to also have either the ROW or COLUMN percentages checked, depending on the data, but in this case check all 3 percentages so you can see what you get and learn about them. Click CONTINUE and OK.

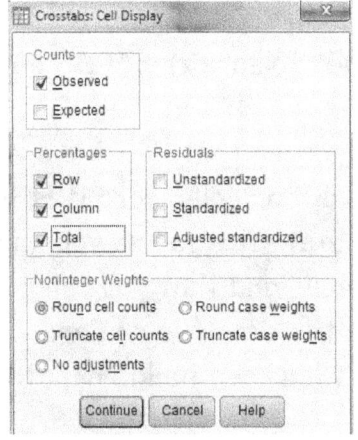

Posted a profile * Course Grade Crosstabulation

			Course Grade				Total
			A	B	C	F	
Posted a profile	NO	Count	2	0	1	0	3
		% within Posted a profile	66.7%	.0%	33.3%	.0%	100.0%
		% within Course Grade	50.0%	.0%	100.0%	.0%	30.0%
		% of Total	20.0%	.0%	10.0%	.0%	30.0%
	YES	Count	2	4	0	1	7
		% within Posted a profile	28.6%	57.1%	.0%	14.3%	100.0%
		% within Course Grade	50.0%	100.0%	.0%	100.0%	70.0%
		% of Total	20.0%	40.0%	.0%	10.0%	70.0%
Total		Count	4	4	1	1	10
		% within Posted a profile	40.0%	40.0%	10.0%	10.0%	100.0%
		% within Course Grade	100.0%	100.0%	100.0%	100.0%	100.0%
		% of Total	40.0%	40.0%	10.0%	10.0%	100.0%

Now let's dissect this.
- Here we see a total of 7 who posted their profile and 3 who did not.
- We also see 4 A's, 4 B's, 1 C and 1 F.
- Of the 3 who did not post a profile, 2 got an A and 1 got a C.
- Of the 7 who did post a profile, 2 got an A, 4 got a B and 1 got an F.
- The % WITHIN POSTED A PROFILE row computes percentages by row, so of the 3 who did not post a profile, 2 got an A (which is 66.7%).
- The % WITHIN COURSE GRADE row computes percentages by column, so of the 4 who got an A, 2 did not post a profile (which is 50.0%).
- The % OF TOTAL row computes percentages of each cell against the overall total, so of the 10 total students, 2 did not post a profile but got an A (which is 20.0%).

You may find it too busy to have all of these percentages or you may find it useful. You may wish to just breakdown the grades within each profile group and so only include the first percentage. Whatever the case, you have complete flexibility. I recommend showing all of them and then deciding what you don't want to see, and then rerunning the table.

Don't forget to save the SPSS output file before you close the session.

You will discover that SPSS is a wonderful tool with a lot of flexibility and capability. The only way to really learn it is to explore and practice. It is important, though, that you learn Statistics too so you know exactly what you are creating, that you are using the data properly, and that you can correctly interpret results. Now that we have explored setting up the data file and analyzing data descriptively, let's move on to inferential statistics where we tackle hypothesis testing, which is at the core of research.

CHAPTER 5: The Basics of Hypothesis Testing

Statistics is one of the scariest subjects for many students at all college levels. Many doctoral learners pursue qualitative dissertations just to avoid the use of statistics, but in today's era of computers and user-friendly statistical software, there is no reason to fear the subject matter. Quantitative studies are typically easier to conduct than qualitative studies because the steps are clear and the results speak for themselves. The key to successful study design is in knowing what you are doing.

The essence of a quantitative study involves hypothesis testing with measurable variables. The vast majority of quantitative studies use only a few types of hypothesis tests.   In this book, I will address how to write a hypothesis correctly, choose the right hypothesis test, set up the test correctly, evaluate the appropriateness of the test, conduct the test using SPSS (a powerful yet easy-to-learn statistical package), interpret the output and write your conclusions in English. Following these clearly laid out guidelines, you'll find that what is often the scariest chapter of the dissertation can be seen as a series of steps that you can follow.

What is a hypothesis? Simply put, a hypothesis is a statement that tests one or two measurable variables, typically asking if there is a difference or a relationship between the variables. The null hypothesis, designated Ho, is a statement of equality or no difference or no relationship (e.g., "the mean age equals 40" OR "the mean weight loss for males equals that of females" OR "there is no relationship between age and salary"). While we can never prove the null hypothesis is a true statement, it is a statement that we assume true in the absence of evidence to the contrary, in the same manner that we assume a defendant is innocent until evidence strongly suggests he/she is guilty or that a patient does not have a medical problem until the tests come back positive. Opposite a null hypothesis is an alternate hypothesis, designated H_A or H_1. The alternate hypothesis is a statement indicating a direction of inequality (i.e., greater than or less than) or a statement of inequality without direction (i.e., not equal to) or a statement indicating that a relationship does exist. When a direction is used, the test is referred to as upper-tailed (>) or lower-tailed (<); when no clear direction is used, the test is referred to as two-tailed (≠). For example, "the mean age > 40" OR "the mean weight loss for males ≠ the mean weight loss for females" OR "there is a relationship between age and salary."

To evaluate the truth of a hypothesis, we conduct a hypothesis test. The output for each hypothesis test has a *Sig. Value* (also known as a *p-value* in statistics books) which measures the probability of such results occurring by random chance. When the p-value is large (i.e., greater than 5%), we consider the results something that can easily happen by chance (for example, you wouldn't jump to the conclusion that a coin will always flip with the head up just because someone flipped heads on the coin three times in a row; three heads in a row can easily happen by chance), while a p-value that is small (i.e., less than 5%) gives us reason to doubt our hypothesis (you would get suspicious if someone rolled the same dice total three times in a row because this doesn't easily happen by chance). Thus we look at the results obtained from a sample and determine if the results are far enough from the hypothesized value that it could only have occurred because the hypothesis is not true or if it is likely to have occurred by random chance. This will be addressed further in the remaining chapters.

The first hurdle is choosing the correct hypothesis test. This requires answering four questions:
1. What is the level of measurement?
2. Can a parametric test be used?
3. How many samples are involved?
4. If two or more samples are involved, are the cases related or independent?

1. What is the level of measurement?
The level of measurement for a variable can be Nominal, Ordinal or Scale.
 ➢ A nominal variable is categorical, and has no order or magnitude. There is no meaning to the variables as numbers. There isn't much you can do with a nominal variable except for counting the frequencies of different values. Examples of nominal variables include Gender or Phone Number (for example, you wouldn't compare how much bigger your phone number is than that of your friend).
 ➢ An ordinal variable has an order of increasing or decreasing value allowing judgment about which is higher than another and recognizing that the values are not consistent (i.e., no magnitude). You can compare ordinal variables by relative position, but you shouldn't average them. Examples would include the Likert Scale (5 = Strongly Agree, 4 = Agree, 3 = Neutral, 2 = Disagree, 1 = Strongly Disagree), the Highest Degree Earned (1 = none, 2 = AA, 3 = BS, 4 = MS, 5 = PhD) or anything with a ranking. Getting a 1 and a 5 on the Likert Scale is not the same as getting a 3 and a 3 (i.e., having a very happy customer and a very angry customer does not equal having two lukewarm customers).
A scale variable has order and magnitude, whereby you can judge what is higher and by how much because the differences are consistent (a dollar is a dollar, a year is a year, etc.). You can also compute averages and make ratio comparisons (like a 40-year old is twice as old as a 20-year old). Examples include Age, Height, Weight, Income, and Years of Experience.

2. Can a parametric test be used?

When the hypothesis involves looking at means or other population computations (known as parameters), we use what is known as a parametric test, and this test has a set of assumptions that must be met. If the assumptions for the parametric test cannot be met, then we can use an alternate approach known as a nonparametric test (not as powerful but little to no assumptions to worry about).

3. How many samples are involved?

The most basic hypothesis test involves looking at a single sample and computing a value from that sample to compare to a hypothesized value. More commonly, we look at two samples to compare a difference or a relationship in some measured value (e.g., compare the mean age for males vs. females). Sometimes you will see three or more samples for which we assess the differences in some measured value (e.g., compare the mean age for married vs. single vs. divorced vs. widowed).

4. If two or more samples are involved, are the cases related or independent?

If multiple samples are used, it is possible that values from one sample are linked to the other(s). The most common occurrence is a pre/post test in which we would compare someone's before and after scores, such as one's weight before and after a diet. Another possibility occurs when the same item is measured under two circumstances, such as having each house appraised by the same two appraisers. Yet another possibility involves manually pairing values based on known information (e.g., pairing husbands with wives, or identical twins, or just two people that are similar in factors the research finds critical). Pairing the samples together makes the test more powerful, but it is not always practical to do and it involves a lot of planning. In this book, this more complex sample pairing is beyond the scope of this presentation.

In this book, we shall look at the six most common hypothesis test options used in research:
- One Sample Test
- Two Sample Test for Independent Samples
- Two Sample Test for Paired Samples
- Multiple Samples Test
- Test of Correlation
- Test of Independence

We will also look at Multiple Regression Analysis, designed for creating models to predict the value of one variable by using several other variables.

Each test type varies by number of samples, levels of measurement, and pairing of samples, and the first five hypothesis tests (identified above) have a parametric and a nonparametric approach available, while the Test of Independence is strictly nonparametric. To truly understand the steps involved with each hypothesis test, let's use a mock database and walk through an example of each hypothesis test.

Go to http://www.DrJimMirabella.com/spss and download the file named **PhDLearners.sav** The file consists of 200 learner records and has 10 variables. Note that this file is 100% fictitious. Let's assume the 200 learners were randomly chosen.

ID	Gender	School	Employ	Age	GPA	Recommend	Comps	Comps_PF	MS_GPA
1	0	1	0	39	2.82	1	14	0	3.05
2	0	1	2	55	3.49	1	33	1	3.45
3	0	1	1	43	3.28	0	34	1	3.50
4	0	1	2	56	3.25	1	35	1	3.55
5	0	1	2	38	3.26	0	31	1	3.30
6	0	1	0	54	2.87	1	18	0	3.05
7	0	1	2	30	3.16	1	32	1	3.35

- ➢ ID is nothing more than a unique identifier for each learner. It has no value in the analysis, yet it is useful in case you need to locate a learner to examine a data discrepancy.
- ➢ GENDER has a value of 0 for Male learners and 1 for Female learners.
- ➢ SCHOOL has a value of 1 if the learner is in the School of Business, 2 for Education, 3 for Human Services and 4 for Psychology.
- ➢ EMPLOY has a value of 0 if the learner is Unemployed, 1 if a Part-Time Employee, and 2 if a Full-Time Employee.
- ➢ AGE is the learner's age in years as of his/her last birthday.
- ➢ GPA is the learner's cumulative GPA to date in the PhD program.
- ➢ RECOMMEND has a value of 1 if the learner indicated in a recent survey that he/she would recommend the PhD program to a friend, and 0 if he/she *would not* recommend the program.
- ➢ COMPS is the learner's score on the Comprehensive Exam, ranging from a minimum of 10 to a maximum of 50, with 30 being a passing grade.
- ➢ COMPS_PF has a value of 1 if the learner passed the Comprehensive Exam by scoring at least 30 points, and 0 if the learner failed by scoring less than 30 points.
- ➢ MS_GPA is the learner's GPA from his/her Masters program.

Now, onto the hypothesis tests. Let the fun begin!

CHAPTER 6: Hypothesis Test for One Sample

In this chapter we shall walk through the steps for conducting a t-Test for One Sample. For this test, a single variable is chosen, a sample mean is computed, and that sample mean is compared to some specified value.

Suppose you wanted to know whether the PhD learners have a mean GPA that differs from 3.50. The null hypothesis (Ho) and alternate hypothesis (Ha) would be:

Ho: The mean GPA of PhD learners equals 3.50

Ha: The mean GPA of PhD learners does not equal 3.50 **(note that the null and alternate are exact opposites of each other → SO many students miss this).**

The only variable being tested here is the GPA. Note that "PhD learners" is <u>not</u> a variable since all of the data being analyzed is from PhD learners (it is merely a descriptor for the target population in this case).

Since we are testing a sample mean against a hypothesized value, we shall use a t-Test for One Sample. To do so, there is an assumption that the GPA is normally distributed.

We really only need to visually check the data to see if it "appears" normal.

Go to *GRAPHS→ LEGACY DIALOGS →* *HISTOGRAM*

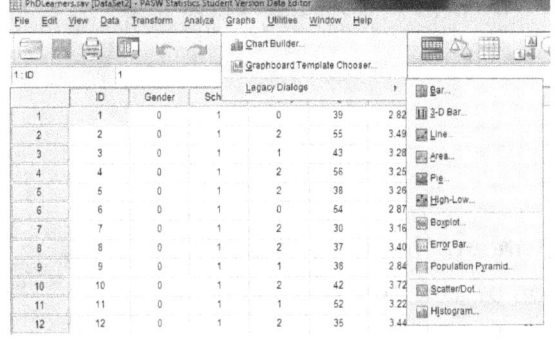

Choose GPA as the VARIABLE by clicking on the arrow to enter it in the box as shown here.

Check the box marked DISPLAY NORMAL CURVE.

Click OK.

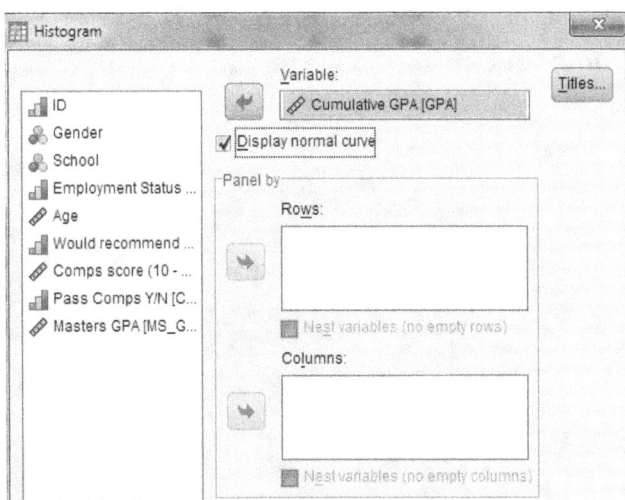

Now a truly normal curve is shaped like a bell that peaks in the middle and is perfectly symmetrical. This histogram does not appear to have a perfect bell-shaped pattern, but I wouldn't expect it to (remember that you are only looking at a sample, not the entire population). There is more data in the middle, and less toward the two extremes. Additionally, it appears that about half of the data are above and half are below the mean. Also, there aren't any unusually large or small numbers at either extreme (known as outliers). Based on these observations, the assumption of normality appears reasonable, so we can proceed with the t-test. If you weren't sure, you could conduct a Kolmogorov-Smirnov test to evaluate the normality assumption.

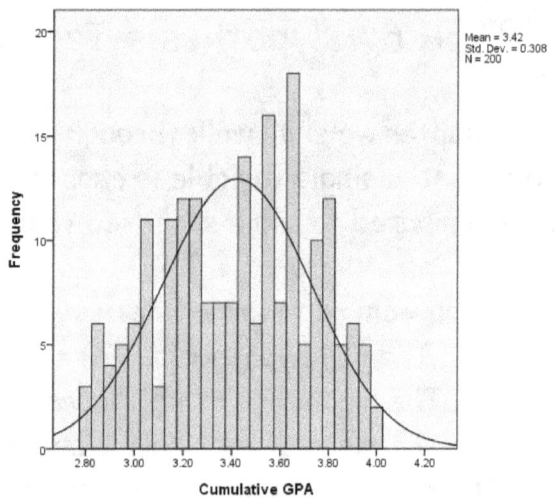

To conduct the Kolmogorov-Smirnov test,
go to ANALYZE →
NONPARAMETRIC TESTS →
ONE SAMPLE

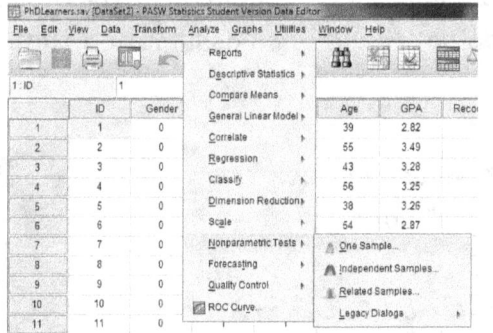

This window (new to the latest version of the software) asks you if you wish to test every variable or specific ones. Click on FIELDS.

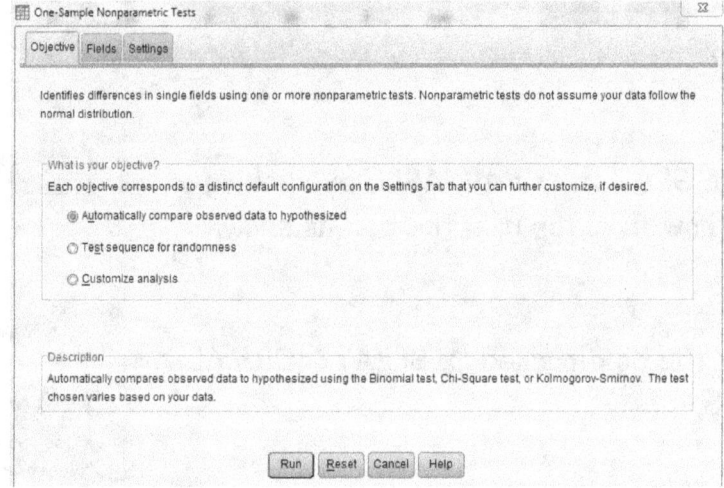

The default is for every variable to be a test field. Choose the USE CUSTOM FIELD ASSIGNMENTS option to remove all of the variables so you can choose the one you want.

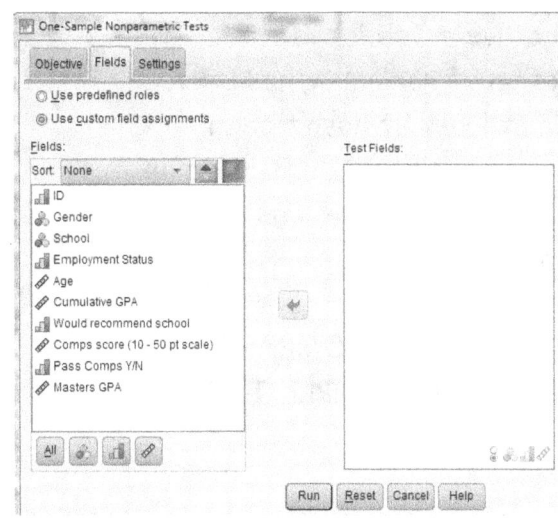

Choose <u>Cumulative GPA</u> and click the arrow so it is moved into the TEST FIELDS.   Then click RUN.

Hypothesis Test Summary

	Null Hypothesis	Test	Sig.	Decision
1	The distribution of Cumulative GPA is normal with mean 3.421 and standard deviation 0.308.	One-Sample Kolmogorov-Smirnov Test	.202	Retain the null hypothesis.

Asymptotic significances are displayed. The significance level is .05.

The hypotheses being tested is

    Ho: The distribution of GPAs is normal.
    Ha: The distribution of GPAs is not normal.

The results show a SIG. value of .202 (this is also known as the p-value). The p-value tells you the probability of getting the results you got if the null were actually true (i.e., it is the probability you would be in error if you rejected the null hypothesis). If the p-value is less than .05, you reject the normality assumption, and if the p-value is greater than .05, there is insufficient evidence to suggest the distribution is not normal (meaning that you can proceed with the assumption of normality). Since the p-value is .202, there is no reason to doubt the distribution is normal, so you can safely proceed with the t-test.

NOTE: While the decision here states RETAIN THE NULL HYPOTHESIS, it is not the best choice of wording. A null hypothesis should never be accepted or retained. We either reject the null hypothesis or fail to reject the null hypothesis, just as a defendant on trial is either found "guilty" (reject the null that he is innocent), or "not guilty" (do not reject the null that he is innocent). He is never found innocent, as there is either enough evidence to convict or insufficient evidence to convict, but he is never proven innocent. Hypothesis testing is all about gathering evidence to suggest the null is not true, and the lack of such evidence warrants a "Do not reject" decision. So throughout this book, I will never RETAIN THE NULL HYPOTHESIS regardless of what the output shows; I will instead FAIL TO REJECT THE NULL HYPOTHESIS. I assure you that this is the standard found in textbooks and academic journals.

Now that we established the assumption of normality has been met (or at least, it hasn't been conclusively violated), let's move on to testing the mean GPA as planned.

Go to ANALYZE → COMPARE MEANS → ONE-SAMPLE T-TEST

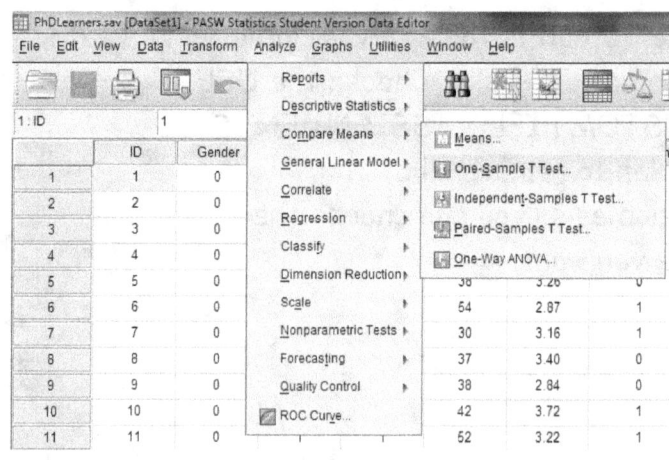

Choose <u>GPA</u> as the TEST VARIABLE and 3.50 as the TEST VALUE. Then click OK.

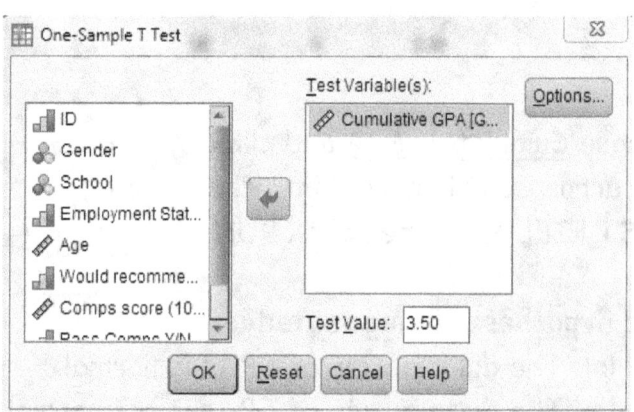

Choose GPA as the TEST VARIABLE and 3.50 as the TEST VALUE. Then click OK.

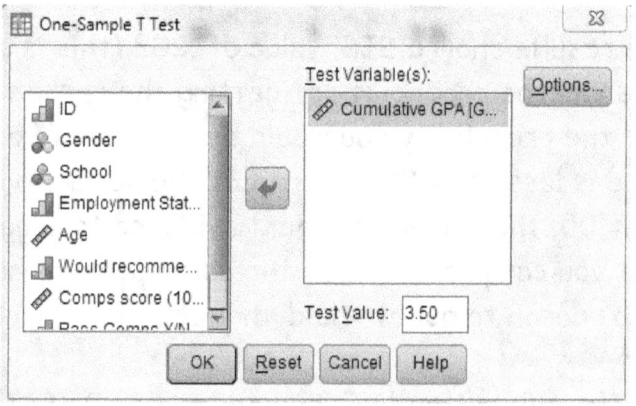

One-Sample Statistics

	N	Mean	Std. Deviation	Std. Error Mean
Cumulative GPA	200	3.4214	.30841	.02181

One-Sample Test

	Test Value = 3.50					
					95% Confidence Interval of the Difference	
	t	df	Sig. (2-tailed)	Mean Difference	Lower	Upper
Cumulative GPA	-3.602	199	.000	-.07855	-.1216	-.0355

The output here shows an *N* of 200 (i.e., the sample size) and a *Mean* of 3.4215 (i.e., the average). The t-test output has a *Sig. (2-tailed)* / p-value of .000. A p-value of .000 means that the probability of a randomly drawing a sample of 200 from a population with a mean of 3.50 and getting a sample mean as low as 3.42 purely by chance is 0.00%. In other words, it is unlikely to have occurred by chance and is more likely the case that the mean is not as hypothesized.

We typically set a significance level at .05, but sometimes we adjust it to as little as .01 or as much as .10. Our decision to adjust it is based on our tolerance for the two types of error (i.e., rejecting the null hypothesis that is true vs. not rejecting a null that is false). For now let's go with .05, which has become a default for most studies. Since the p-value is less than .05 (our chosen significance level), we reject the null. When we reject the null, we are basically declaring the alternate hypothesis to be true; when we fail to reject the null, we state that there is insufficient evidence to declare the alternate hypothesis to be true (but you need to write in accordance with the wording of the specific hypothesis instead of just making a generic statement about the null or alternate, as shown in the next paragraph).

Had we not rejected the null hypothesis, we would state that there is insufficient evidence to conclude the mean GPA differs from 3.50. Remember that under no circumstances should you ever "accept" the null and/or conclude the mean equals 3.50 as it is impossible to prove the null is true (and think about how silly it would be if you had a sample mean of 3.55 which wasn't quite large enough to reject the null, and so you concluded that the mean was therefore exactly 3.50, which is smaller than your sample mean).

As for this case of testing the GPA, however, we did reject the null hypothesis, so we should conclude that the mean GPA of PhD learners differs from 3.50. Since the sample mean is 3.42, we can get more specific and state that the mean GPA is less than 3.50.

At this point, I recommend going one extra step with the conclusion. Does it make sense? What does it really mean? In this case, you might state that, contrary to rumors, grades do not appear to be inflated, as the mean GPA leans closer to the B range than to the A range. Anything more should be saved for Chapter 5 of your dissertation, when you tie the results to the literature and make suggestions for future research.

Now what if the normality assumption did not hold up, or the sample size was relatively small (often considered to mean less than 30 per sample)? In such cases, you can conduct a nonparametric test that essentially tests the same principle without the parameter (i.e., the mean) and without the assumptions. In this case, we shall use a Binomial test.

To conduct the Binomial test, go to ANALYZE → NONPARAMETRIC TESTS → ONE SAMPLE. Then click on FIELDS and choose the USE CUSTOM FIELD ASSIGNMENTS option. Select <u>Cumulative GPA</u> as the TEST FIELD. Then click on SETTINGS.

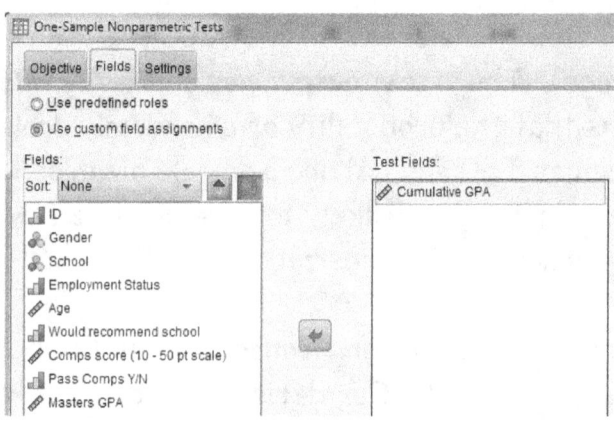

Choose CUSTOMIZE TESTS and check the first box to run the BINOMIAL TEST. We skipped this before because it automatically ran the test for normality, but now we need to tell it what we want done. Click on OPTIONS.

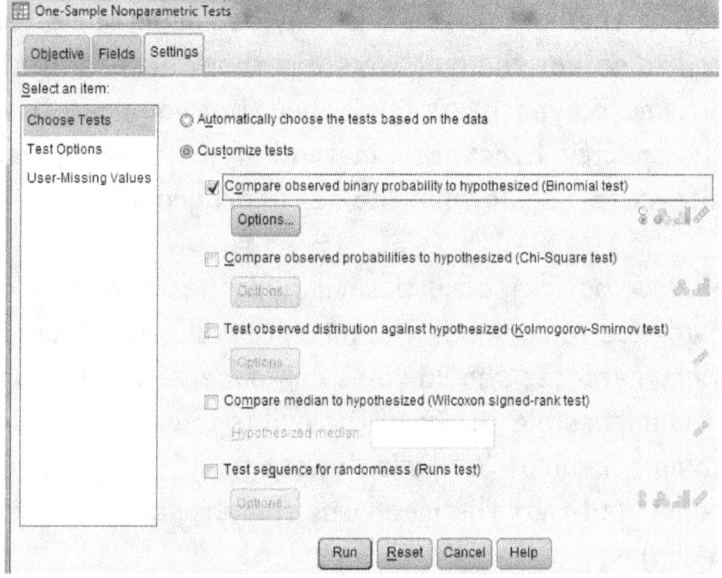

The HYPOTHESIZED PROPORTION is already set to a default of .50, which is want we want. In the bottom right, choose CUSTOM CUT POINT and enter 3.50. This will test if 50% of the GPAs are above 3.50 and 50% are below. In a normal distribution where the mean is 3.50, you would expect to see a perfect 50/50 split, so this is essentially the equivalent without testing the mean. Click OK and RUN.

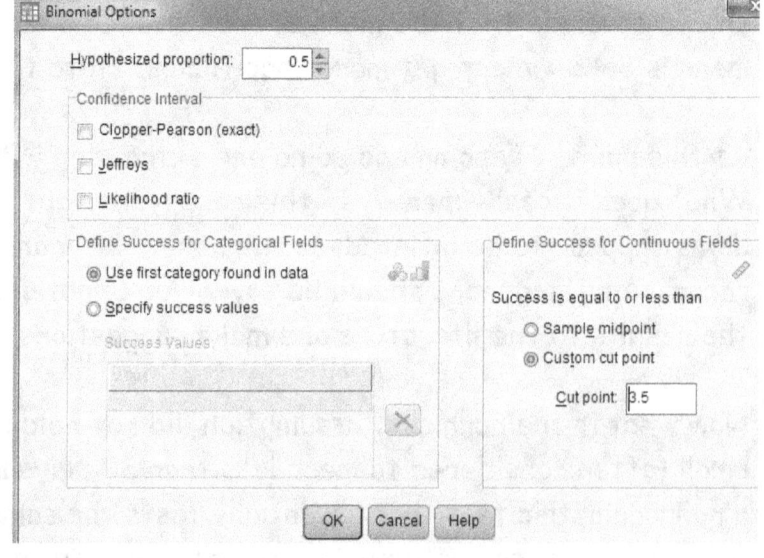

The output here shows that the GPA was broken down into two groups: <= 3.5 and > 3.5 56% of the GPAs are less than 3.5 and 44% are greater. If the mean were 3.50 and the distribution were normal, you would expect to see 50% above / below 3.50.

Hypothesis Test Summary

	Null Hypothesis	Test	Sig.	Decision
1	The categories defined by Cumulative GPA <=3.5 and >3.5 occur with probabilities 0.5 and 0.5.	One-Sample Binomial Test	.138	Retain the null hypothesis.

Asymptotic significances are displayed. The significance level is .05.

If the mean were 3.50 and the distribution were normal, you would expect to see 50% above / below 3.50. The p-value of .138 is greater than .05, so the null hypothesis is not rejected and there is insufficient evidence to conclude that the percentage of GPAs above 3.50 is not 50%. Notice that the t-test resulted in rejecting Ho, while the Binomial test did not. This is not unusual. A parametric test (like the t-test) is more powerful and more capable of detecting significant differences, while a nonparametric test (like the Binomial test) is weaker and more conservative in its likelihood of finding a difference to be significant. This is why we try to use parametric tests whenever possible, but when it is not an option, at least we have a viable alternative, albeit a little weaker.

Now what if you wish to see more than just the HYPOTHESIS TEST SUMMARY? Personally I prefer to see the entire output so I can draw more detailed conclusions. Here's how.

To conduct the Binomial test, go to ANALYZE → NONPARAMETRIC TESTS → LEGACY DIALOGS → BINOMIAL.

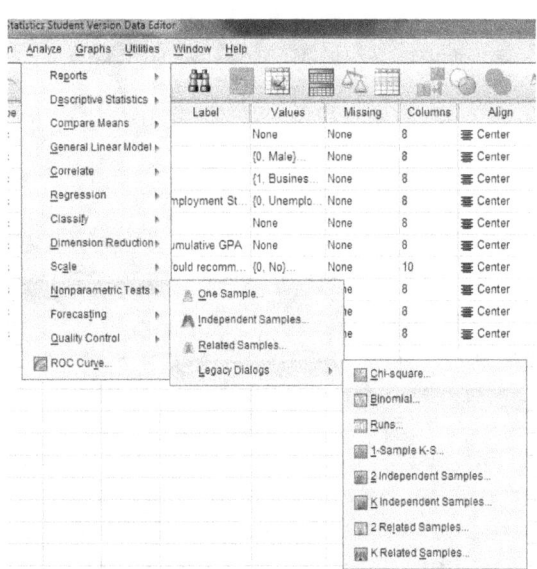

Choose <u>Cumulative GPA</u> as the
TEST VARIABLE. Set the CUT
POINT to 3.50 and the TEST
PROPORTION to 0.50 since we are
testing if half of the data are
above / below 3.50. Click OK.

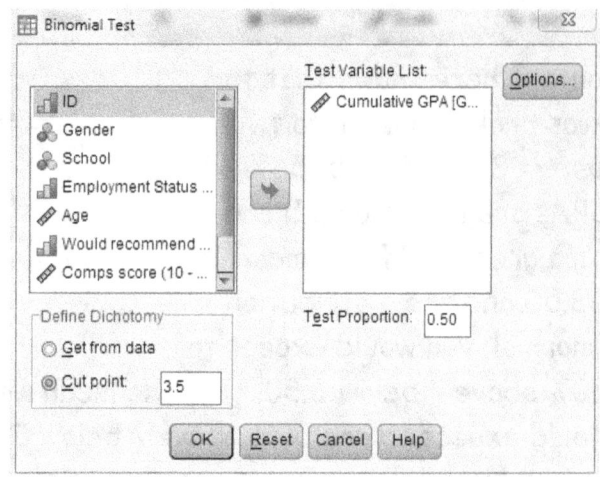

Here we get to see that 111 of the
200 were below 3.50 and the other
89 were above 3.50. The ASYMP.
SIG. (2-TAILED) of .137 is greater
than .05, so we fail to reject the

		Category	N	Observed Prop.	Test Prop.	Asymp. Sig. (2-tailed)
Cumulative GPA	Group 1	<= 3.5	111	.56	.50	.137[a]
	Group 2	> 3.5	89	.44		
	Total		200	1.00		
a. Based on Z Approximation.						

Binomial Test

null hypothesis. Personally I prefer this to the other display (especially since it
erroneously uses the RETAIN word), and you will need this for journals or dissertations,
but you can do whatever works for you. SPSS is great in that it gives you many options.

So let's review.

```
State the hypotheses:
     Ho:  The mean GPA of PhD learners equals 3.50
     Ha:  The mean GPA of PhD learners does not equal 3.50

Choose a significance level → .05

State the assumption(s):
     PhD GPAs are normally distributed.
     → evaluate graphically or with a Kolmogorov-Smirnov test

Conduct t-Test for One Sample

Compare the sig.value / p-value to .05. If greater than .05, do not
reject Ho and then state that there is insufficient evidence to
conclude the mean GPA differs from 3.50. If less than .05, reject Ho
and conclude that the mean GPA in the PhD program is not 3.50
(specify whether it is greater or less than 3.50). Then feel free to
add some insights in English, but be careful not to overstate beyond
what you tested.

If the normality assumption does not hold, conduct a Binomial test
with the following hypothesis →
     Ho: The GPAs of PhD learners are distributed with 50% above 3.50
```

CHAPTER 7: Hypothesis Test for Two Independent Samples

In this chapter we shall walk through the steps for conducting a t-Test for Two Independent Samples. For this test, a single scale variable (the dependent variable) is compared across two subgroups of a nominal or ordinal variable (the independent variable).

Suppose you wanted to know whether there is a difference in the mean GPA for males vs. females in the PhD program. The null hypothesis (Ho) and alternate hypothesis (Ha) would be:

> Ho: The mean GPA of male PhD learners equals that of female PhD learners
>
> Ha: The mean GPA of male PhD learners does not equal that of female PhD learners.

The dependent variable here is the GPA. The independent variable is GENDER with two possible values ("Male" or "Female").

Since we are comparing sample means between two independent groups, we use a t-Test for Two Independent Samples. To do so, there are a few assumptions:

> ➤ The GPAs are normally distributed (this was addressed in Chapter 2)
> ➤ The GPAs are independent (meaning that one learner's GPA is not linked to another learner's GPA). This assumption cannot be tested, but the researcher can make this assumption based on knowledge of the data or the methodology used for collecting the data.
> ➤ The "males" and "females" are independent groups (meaning that we are treating the "males" as a single group and the "females" as a single group, and that there isn't a direct link between individual "males" and "females"). If the data consisted of husbands in one group and their wives in the other, this assumption would be violated. This assumption cannot be tested, so it is up to the researcher to confirm the independence of the groups.
> ➤ The distribution of GPAs for "males" vs. "females" have equal variances (this can be evaluated graphically or tested statistically). The good news is that while this assumption could be violated, the t-test can overcome it.

Since we have already addressed the normality assumption for GPAs in chapter 2, let's look at the assumption of equal variances. First let's create a boxplot.

Go to GRAPHS → LEGACY DIALOGS → BOXPLOT

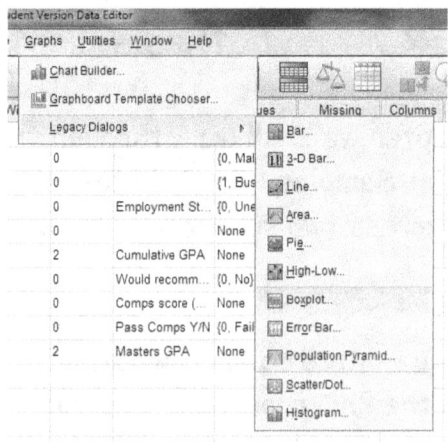

Choose SIMPLE and click DEFINE.

Choose <u>Cumulative GPA</u> as the VARIABLE (vertical Y-Axis) and <u>Gender</u> as the CATEGORY AXIS *(horizontal X-Axis)* since we are showing the distribution of GPAs by Gender. Then OK.

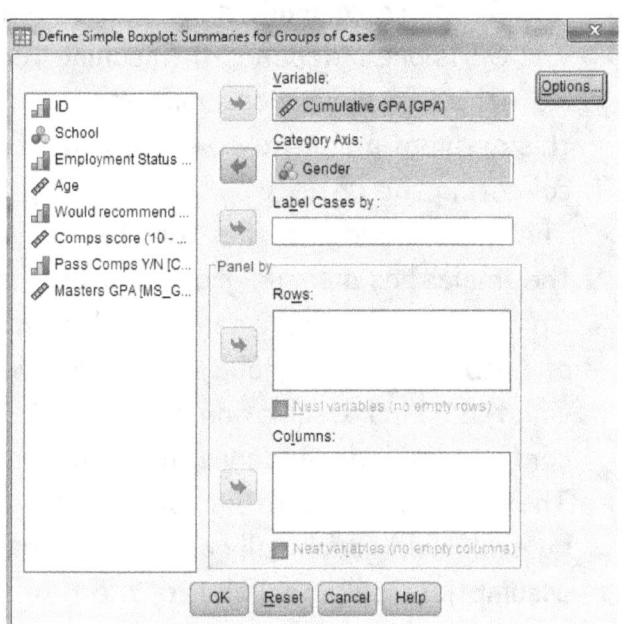

The boxplot shows the spread of GPAs for "males" vs. "females". You can see the boxes are about the same size, and the size of the whiskers are also about the same size, so it appears that the variability is similar for the two Genders. We may now proceed with the t-test. Now if the assumption didn't hold up, the good news is that the t-test is robust enough to handle this assumption being violated. Let's take a look.

To conduct the t-Test for Two Independent Samples, go to ANALYZE → COMPARE MEANS → INDEPENDENT SAMPLES T TEST

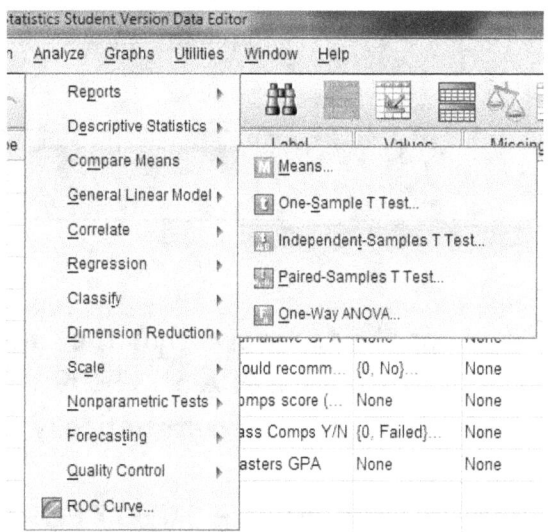

Select <u>Cumulative GPA</u> as the TEST VARIABLE and <u>Gender</u> as the GROUPING VARIABLE.

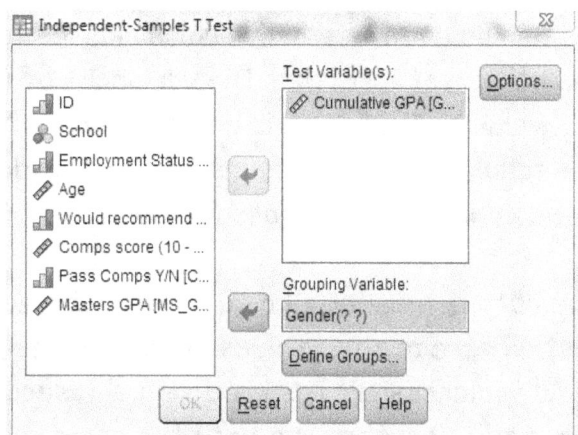

Now choose DEFINE GROUPS so that we can tell SPSS which two groups to compare. In this case, the two groups are "males" and "females" represented by the values of 0 and 1, respectively. Click CONTINUE and OK.

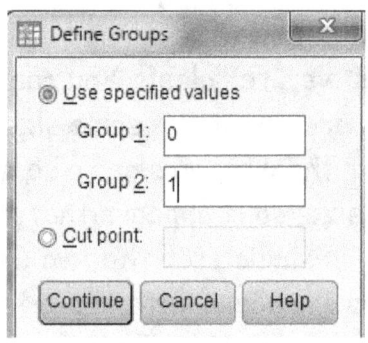

Group Statistics

	Gender	N	Mean	Std. Deviation	Std. Error Mean
Cumulative GPA	Male	100	3.3270	.30137	.03014
	Female	100	3.5159	.28696	.02870

Independent Samples Test

		Levene's Test for Equality of Variances		t-test for Equality of Means						95% Confidence Interval of the Difference	
		F	Sig.	t	df	Sig. (2-tailed)	Mean Difference	Std. Error Difference	Lower	Upper
Cumulative GPA	Equal variances assumed	.461	.498	-4.539	198	.000	-.18890	.04161	-.27096	-.10684
	Equal variances not assumed			-4.539	197.527	.000	-.18890	.04161	-.27096	-.10684

The table at the top shows that the "males" have a mean GPA of 3.327, while the "females" have a mean GPA of 3.5159. Yes there is a difference, but do not judge it unless you prove it to be a statistically significant difference.

Notice under the LEVENE'S TEST FOR EQUALITY OF VARIANCES there is a column with the F statistic and a column with a Sig. value / p-value. That Sig. value is used to determine whether the "equal variances" assumption holds. Essentially, you are testing the null hypothesis that the variances of GPAs are equal for the two Genders. Since the Sig. value = .498 which is greater than .05, we do not reject the null that the variances are equal. Thus there is insufficient evidence to conclude the variances are not equal and so we can comfortably assume equal variances for the t-test.

The output table also has a column labeled SIG. (2-TAILED); this is the p-value for the t-test. There are two values in that column; the first row of numbers is what you use if equal variances are assumed, and the second row is used if equal variances are not assumed. Yes, they are both the same values, but that is just a coincidence; most of the time, they are different values. In this case, we would use the first row, so the p-value is .000 which is less than .05. Thus we would reject Ho and conclude that there is a difference in the mean GPA for "males" vs. "females" in the PhD program. We can even state that females in the PhD program have a higher mean GPA than the males.

Be careful with your conclusions beyond this point. Yes you have demonstrated that females have significantly higher GPAs than the males, but that doesn't make females smarter or better students. It could be that females are predominantly enrolled in an easier program (if such a thing exists). The point is that you don't know the "why" as of yet, which is why we suggest future research to investigate the causes or other factors that might explain or clarify the results.

Now what if the normality assumption did not hold up or the sample size was relatively small? Then you would use the nonparametric equivalent known as the Mann-Whitney test which tests for a difference in the distributions of GPAs for the two Genders.

To conduct the Mann-Whitney test, go to ANALYZE → NONPARAMETRIC TESTS → LEGACY DIALOGS → 2 INDEPENDENT SAMPLES.

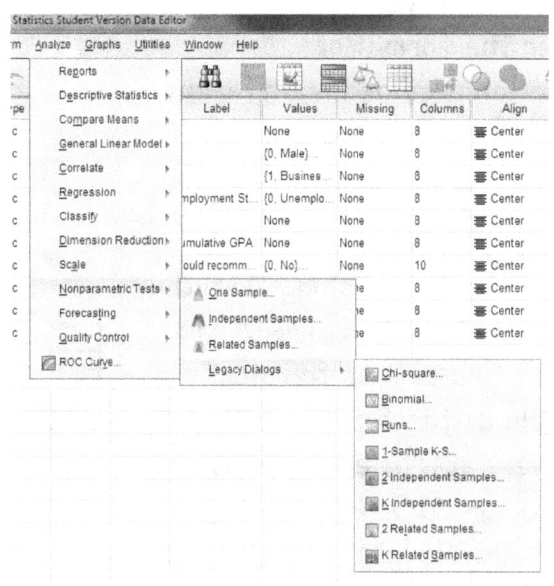

Choose GPA as the TEST VARIABLE, choose Gender for the GROUPING VARIABLE, and check the MANN WHITNEY U box.

Now choose *Define Groups* so that we can tell SPSS which two groups to compare.

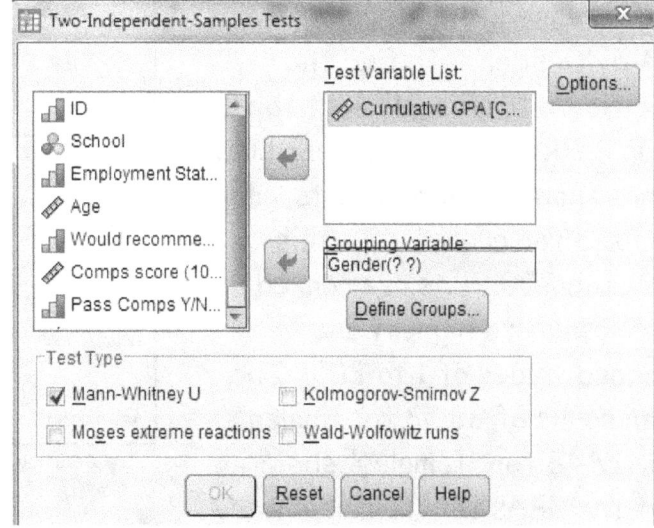

In this case, the two groups are "males" and "females" represented by the values of 0 and 1, respectively.   Click CONTINUE.

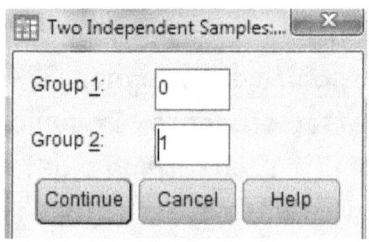

If you would like, you may click OPTIONS and choose DESCRIPTIVE STATISTICS. You already have this information, but sometimes it is great to see whether the format or information provided is different from what you have already seen. Click CONTINUE and OK.

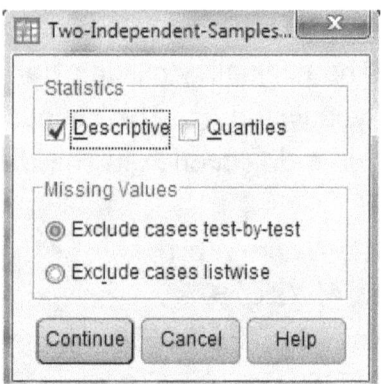

The null hypothesis being tested is that the distribution of GPA's is equal for "males" vs. "females." The table at the top shows that there were 100 of each GENDER. The ASYMP. SIG. (2-TAILED) value of .000 is less than .05, thus you would reject Ho and conclude a difference in the distribution of GPA by Gender.   To find the specific difference, look at the Mean Rank for each Gender. Like in most nonparametric tests, ranks are used for analysis. In this case, the 200 GPAs are ranked from lowest to highest and assigned values of 1 to 200. The mean ranks of 83.53 for "males" and 117.48 for "females" shows that the GPAs for "females" were higher as a whole. Thus you would conclude that "females" have higher GPAs than "males" in the PhD program. .

Descriptive Statistics

	N	Mean	Std. Deviation	Minimum	Maximum
Cumulative GPA	200	3.4215	.30841	2.80	3.99
Gender	200	.50	.501	0	1

Mann-Whitney Test

Ranks

	Gender	N	Mean Rank	Sum of Ranks
Cumulative GPA	Male	100	83.53	8352.50
	Female	100	117.48	11747.50
	Total	200		

Test Statistics[a]

	Cumulative GPA
Mann-Whitney U	3302.500
Wilcoxon W	8352.500
Z	-4.148
Asymp. Sig. (2-tailed)	.000

a. Grouping Variable: Gender

There is a shortcut to the Mann Whitney test, but it does lack info (and this is the case for the other nonparametric tests, so I won't go through all of the other shortcuts). Go to ANALYZE → NONPARAMETRIC TESTS → INDEPENDENT SAMPLES.

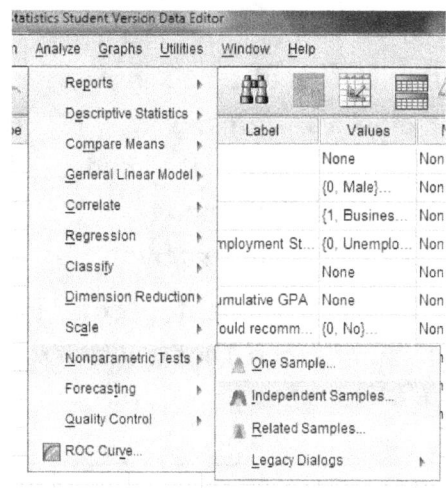

Choose the AUTOMATICALLY COMPARE DISTRIBUTIONS ACROSS GROUPS as your objective. Then click on FIELDS and choose the USE CUSTOM FIELD ASSIGNMENTS option.

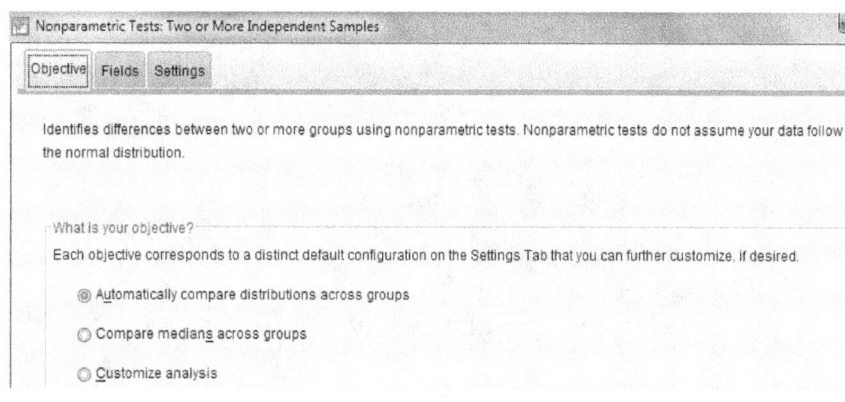

Choose Cumulative GPA as the TEST FIELD and choose Gender for the GROUPS. Then click on RUN.

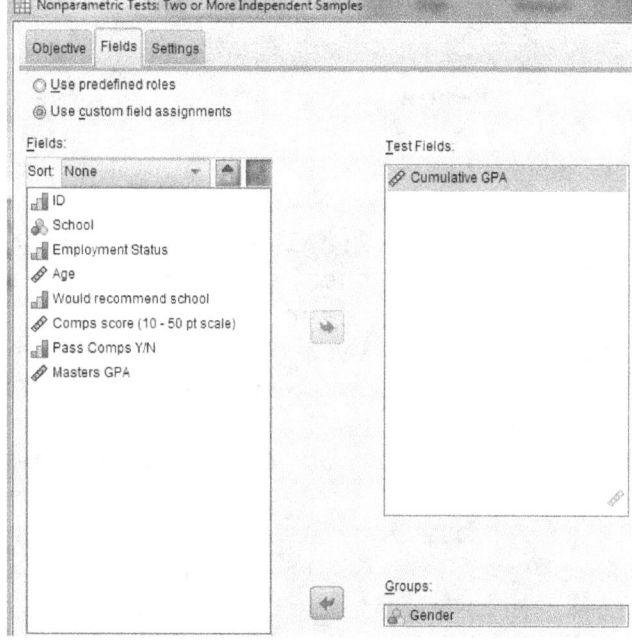

The null hypothesis being tested is that the distribution of GPA's is equal for "males" vs. "females." The null hypothesis is rejected and it can be concluded that the distribution of GPAs differs by

Hypothesis Test Summary

	Null Hypothesis	Test	Sig.	Decision
1	The distribution of Cumulative GPA is the same across categories of Gender.	Independent-Samples Mann-Whitney U Test	.000	Reject the null hypothesis.

Asymptotic significances are displayed. The significance level is .05.

gender. If that is sufficient, great! Personally I prefer the other method so I can see the actual numbers, and that will be critical in journals and dissertations.

So let's review.

```
State the hypotheses:
      Ho:  The mean GPA of male PhD learners equals that of female PhD
           learners
      Ha:  The mean GPA of male PhD learners does not equal that of
           female PhD learners.

Choose a significance level → .05

State the assumption(s):
      PhD GPAs are normally distributed.
      → evaluate graphically or with a Kolmogorov-Smirnov test

      PhD GPAs are independent.
      → must be confirmed by the researcher

      Males and Females in the PhD program are independent.
      → must be confirmed by the researcher

      GPAs for males vs. females have equal variances.
      → evaluated graphically or with Levene's test
      → t-test can handle this assumption being violated.

Conduct t-Test for Two Independent Samples

Compare the sig.value / p-value to .05.  If greater than .05, do not
reject Ho and then state that there is insufficient evidence to
conclude a difference in the mean GPA for male vs. female PhD
learners.  If less than .05, reject Ho and conclude that the mean
GPAs for males and females in the PhD program are not equal (specify
which was greater); then feel free to add some insights in English,
but be careful not to overstate beyond what you tested.

If the normality assumption does not hold, conduct a Mann-Whitney
test with the following hypothesis →
      Ho: The distribution of GPAs of PhD learners is the same for
          males vs. females.
```

CHAPTER 8: Hypothesis Test for Paired Samples

In this chapter we shall walk through the steps for conducting a t-Test for Paired Samples. For this test, a scale variable (the dependent variable) is taken under two conditions (the independent variable) and compared one row at a time. Unlike the test for Independent Samples where the overall mean for one group is compared to the overall mean for another, here the individual differences are computed row by row and then those differences are analyzed.

Suppose you wanted to know whether there is a difference between the mean PhD GPA vs. the mean Masters GPA for learners in the PhD program. The null hypothesis (Ho) and alternate hypothesis (Ha) would be:

    Ho: There is no difference in the mean PhD GPA vs. the mean Masters GPA for PhD learners.

    Ha: There is a difference in the mean PhD GPA vs. the mean Masters GPA for PhD learners.

The dependent variable here is the GPA. The independent variable is the Degree (with values of "PhD" or "Masters").

Since we are comparing sample means between two related groups (i.e., two different GPAs for the same learner), we use a t-Test for Paired Samples. To do so, there is an assumption that the GPA is normally distributed (refer back to Chapter 6).

To conduct the t-Test for Paired Samples, go to ANALYZE → COMPARE MEANS → PAIRED-SAMPLES T TEST

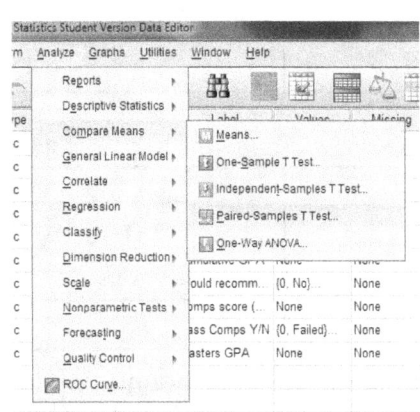

Highlight the <u>Cumulative GPA</u> and <u>Masters_GPA</u> variables and click on the arrow so that they become the PAIRED VARIABLES.

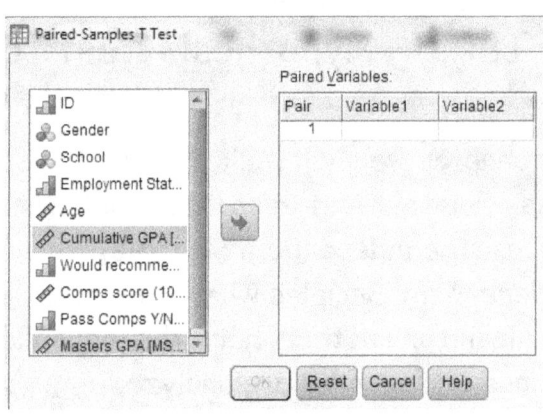

Now click OK.

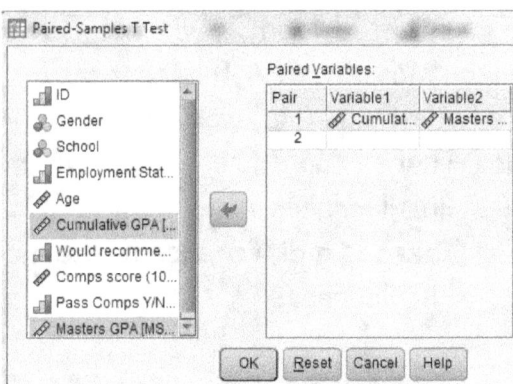

Paired Samples Statistics

		Mean	N	Std. Deviation	Std. Error Mean
Pair 1	Cumulative GPA	3.4214	200	.30841	.02181
	Masters GPA	3.5250	200	.28904	.02044

Paired Samples Correlations

		N	Correlation	Sig.
Pair 1	Cumulative GPA & Masters GPA	200	.925	.000

Paired Samples Test

| | | Paired Differences | | | | | | | |
| | | | | | 95% Confidence Interval of the Difference | | | | |
		Mean	Std. Deviation	Std. Error Mean	Lower	Upper	t	df	Sig. (2-tailed)
Pair 1	Cumulative GPA - Masters GPA	-.10355	.11744	.00830	-.11993	-.08717	-12.469	199	.000

The first table shows the mean Cumulative PhD GPA to be 3.4215, and the mean Masters GPA to be 3.5250. The second table shows the two GPAs to have a correlation of .925; while this is not a test of correlation, this statistic could prove useful when assessing the reliability of a survey question (but this is not the case here). The third table shows the results of the t-test. As is always the case, go straight to the SIG. (2-TAILED) value of .000 which is less than .05, so you would reject Ho and conclude there is a difference in the PhD vs. Masters GPA. Since the sample mean is higher at the Masters level, you could conclude that PhD learners had higher GPAs in their Masters program than they do in their current PhD program. There is nothing else in the data file to suggest why this would be the case; all you can do is suppose why it is true and suggest future research to investigate the theory. Now what if the normality assumption did not hold up or the sample size was relatively small? Then you would use the nonparametric equivalent known as the Wilcoxon Signed-Rank test which tests for whether the difference between one's Masters and PhD GPAs equal zero.

To conduct the Wilcoxon test, go to ANALYZE → NONPARAMETRIC TESTS → LEGACY DIALOGS → 2 RELATED SAMPLES. Highlight the Cumulative GPA and Masters GPA variables and click on the arrow so that they become the TEST PAIR. Check the WILCOXON box. If you would like, you may click OPTIONS and choose DESCRIPTIVE STATISTICS. You already have this information, but

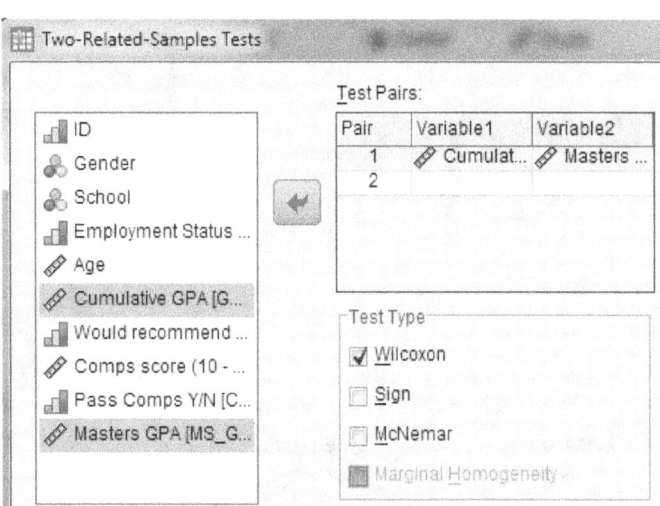

sometimes it is great to see whether the format or information provided is different from what you have already seen. Click OK.

The null hypothesis being tested is that the difference between one's Masters and PhD GPAs equals zero. The ASYMP. SIG. (2-TAILED) value of .000 is less than .05, thus you would reject Ho and conclude a difference in the Masters vs. PhD GPA by learner. To find the specific difference, look at the MEAN RANKS. Since the table shows Masters GPA – Cumulative GPA, a positive value indicates a higher

Wilcoxon Signed Ranks Test

Ranks

		N	Mean Rank	Sum of Ranks
Masters GPA - Cumulative GPA	Negative Ranks	33[a]	51.42	1697.00
	Positive Ranks	160[b]	106.40	17024.00
	Ties	7[c]		
	Total	200		

a. Masters GPA < Cumulative GPA

b. Masters GPA > Cumulative GPA

c. Masters GPA = Cumulative GPA

Test Statistics[b]

	Masters GPA - Cumulative GPA
Z	-9.865[a]
Asymp. Sig. (2-tailed)	.000

a. Based on negative ranks.

b. Wilcoxon Signed Ranks Test

Masters GPA, while a negative value indicates a higher PhD GPA. The POSITIVE RANKS had a MEAN RANK of 106.40 which is much larger than that of the NEGATIVE RANKS, which was 51.42. Thus learners had a significantly higher GPA at the Masters level than at the PhD level.

So let's review.

State the hypotheses:
     Ho: There is no difference in the mean PhD GPA vs. the mean Masters GPA for PhD learners.
     Ha: There is a difference in the mean PhD GPA vs. the mean Masters GPA for PhD learners.

Choose a significance level → .05

State the assumption(s):
     PhD GPAs are normally distributed.
     → evaluate graphically or with a Kolmogorov-Smirnov test

Conduct t-Test for Paired Samples

Compare the sig.value / p-value to .05. If greater than .05, do not reject Ho and then state that there is insufficient evidence to conclude a difference between the Masters and PhD GPAs for the PhD learners. If less than .05, reject Ho and conclude that PhD learners do not have equal GPAs in their Masters and PhD programs (specify which was greater); then feel free to add some insights in English, but be careful not to overstate beyond what you tested.

If the normality assumption does not hold, conduct a Wilcoxon Signed-Rank test with the following hypothesis →
     Ho: the difference between one's Masters and PhD GPAs equals Zero.

CHAPTER 9: Hypothesis Test for Multiple Samples

In this chapter we shall walk through the steps for conducting a One-Way Analysis of Variance. For this test, a single scale variable (the dependent variable) is compared across three or more subgroups of a nominal or ordinal variable (the independent variable).

Suppose you wanted to know whether there is a difference in the mean GPA for learners who are employed full-time vs. part-time vs. unemployed. The null hypothesis (Ho) and alternate hypothesis (Ha) would be:

Ho: There is no difference in the mean GPA for PhD learners as a function of their employment status.

Ha: There is a difference in the mean GPA for PhD learners as a function of their employment status.

The dependent variable here is the GPA. The independent variable is EMPLOYMENT STATUS with three possible values (Full-Time or Part-Time or Unemployed).

Since we are comparing sample means between three or more independent groups, we use a One-Way Analysis of Variance (ANOVA). To do so, there are a few assumptions we must consider:

➢ The GPAs for each employment group are normally distributed (this was addressed in Chapter 2)
➢ The three employment groups are independent (meaning that we are treating the full-timers, part-timers and unemployed as three distinct groups and there isn't a direct link between individuals in any of the groups. This assumption cannot be tested, so it is up to the researcher to confirm this group assignment is appropriate.
➢ The distribution of GPAs for the three employment groups have equal variances (this was addressed in Chapter 3). The good news is that this assumption could be violated and yet the ANOVA can overcome it.

Since we have already addressed the normality assumption for GPAs in chapter 6, we can forego it here, as the procedure is the same. As for the equal variances assumption, you can generate a boxplot as instructed in chapter 7. As you can see, it is difficult to make a call that variances are significantly different (you wouldn't expect them to really be identical, but you want them to be similar). So let's proceed with the ANOVA.

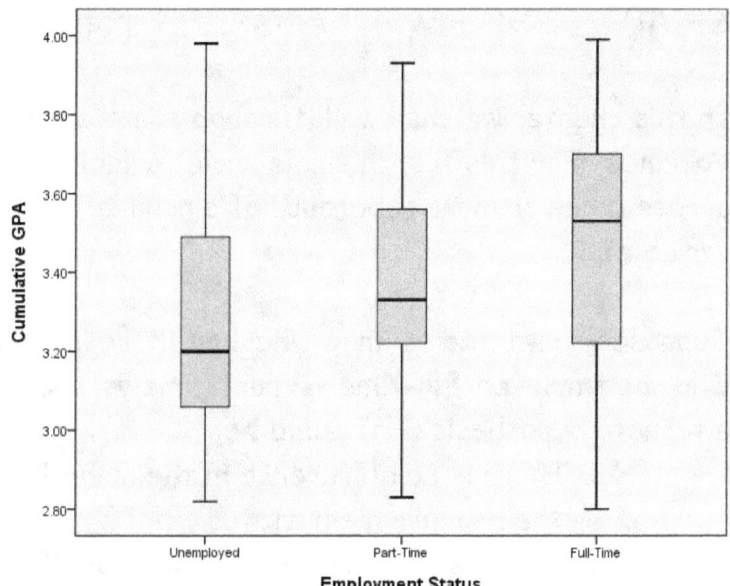

To conduct the Analysis of Variance, go to ANALYZE → COMPARE MEANS → ONE-WAY ANOVA

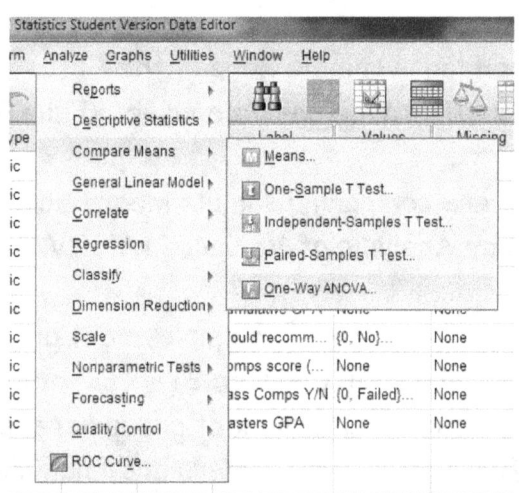

Select Cumulative GPA as the DEPENDENT VARIABLE and Employ as the FACTOR. Then choose OPTIONS.

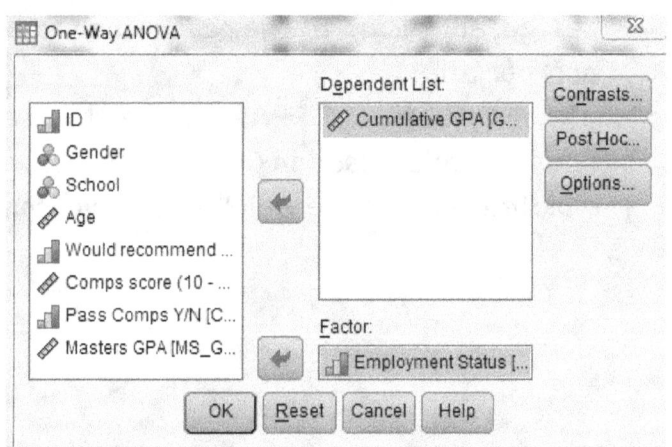

Choose DESCRIPTIVE and HOMOGENEITY OF VARIANCE TEST. This will give you the descriptive statistics if you didn't already have them and will run a test for equal variances. Then CONTINUE. Now select POST HOC.

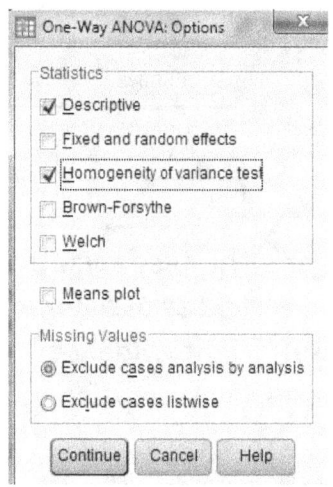

If the results of the ANOVA are significant, it merely tells you that a difference exists somewhere, but you don't know where. You need to perform a Post Hoc test after the fact to see which pairs are significantly different. You can choose any of the 14 tests shown for equal variances (I usually choose BONFERRONI, but they are all fine). Notice that there are 4 tests that can be used if Equal Variances are Not assumed; you can ignore this for now and come back to it if the Equal

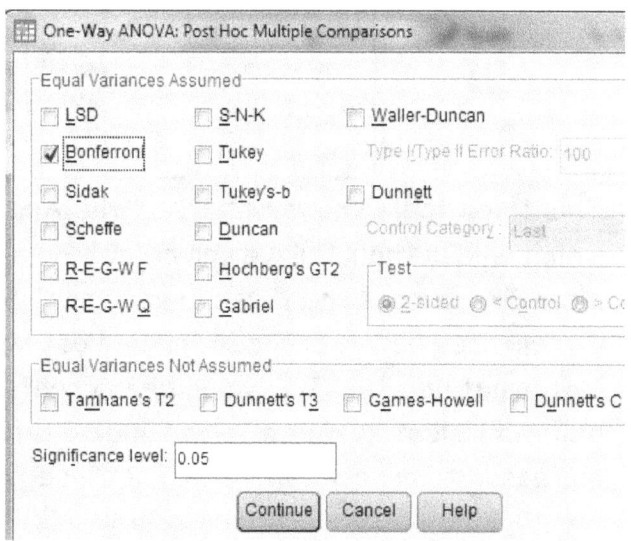

Variances assumption doesn't hold up OR you can just choose one now (I usually choose GAMES-HOWELL). Then CONTINUE and OK.

Descriptives

Cumulative GPA

	N	Mean	Std. Deviation	Std. Error	95% Confidence Interval for Mean		Minimum	Maximum
					Lower Bound	Upper Bound		
Unemployed	25	3.2844	.33173	.06635	3.1475	3.4213	2.82	3.98
Part-Time	45	3.3789	.29139	.04344	3.2913	3.4664	2.83	3.93
Full-Time	130	3.4625	.30220	.02650	3.4101	3.5150	2.80	3.99
Total	200	3.4215	.30841	.02181	3.3784	3.4645	2.80	3.99

This first table shows the Descriptive Statistics of the GPAs for each Employment Status.

Test of Homogeneity of Variances

Cumulative GPA

Levene Statistic	df1	df2	Sig.
.325	2	197	.723

This second table shows the test results for the Levene's test. As with the t-test, here we test for the equal variances assumption. Since the SIG. value is .723 which is greater than .05, there is insufficient evidence to reject the "equal variances" assumption. Thus we can confidently use the assumption of equal variances.

ANOVA

Cumulative GPA

	Sum of Squares	df	Mean Square	F	Sig.
Between Groups	.771	2	.385	4.180	.017
Within Groups	18.158	197	.092		
Total	18.928	199			

This third table shows results of the Analysis of Variance. With a SIG. value of .017 which is less than .05, we can reject Ho and conclude that there is a difference in the mean GPA across the three Employment Status groups. To find where the specific differences lie, we proceed to the Post Hoc test that we chose (in this case, *Bonferroni*). Note that had the SIG. value been greater than .05, we would not reject Ho, there would be insufficient evidence to conclude a difference in the mean GPAs, and there would be no reason to proceed with the Post Hoc test.

Multiple Comparisons

Dependent Variable: Cumulative GPA

	(I) Employment Status	(J) Employment Status	Mean Difference (I-J)	Std. Error	Sig.	95% Confidence Interval	
						Lower Bound	Upper Bound
Bonferroni	Unemployed	Part-Time	-.09449	.07573	.641	-.2773	.0884
		Full-Time	-.17814*	.06630	.023	-.3382	-.0180
	Part-Time	Unemployed	.09449	.07573	.641	-.0884	.2773
		Full-Time	-.08365	.05251	.338	-.2104	.0431
	Full-Time	Unemployed	.17814*	.06630	.023	.0180	.3382
		Part-Time	.08365	.05251	.338	-.0431	.2104
Games-Howell	Unemployed	Part-Time	-.09449	.07930	.464	-.2868	.0978
		Full-Time	-.17814*	.07144	.046	-.3537	-.0026
	Part-Time	Unemployed	.09449	.07930	.464	-.0978	.2868
		Full-Time	-.08365	.05089	.233	-.2052	.0379
	Full-Time	Unemployed	.17814*	.07144	.046	.0026	.3537
		Part-Time	.08365	.05089	.233	-.0379	.2052

*. The mean difference is significant at the 0.05 level.

This fourth table shows results of the BONFERRONI Post Hoc test (disregard the GAMES-HOWELL results since we were able to assume equal variances). Look for the asterisks next to the MEAN DIFFERENCE (I-J) values, as this tells you which pairs are significant (i.e., SIG. less than .05). There is a significant difference between the GPAs for "Unemployed" vs. "Full-Time", with the MEAN DIFFERENCE equal to .17814 and the SIG. value equal to .023. The MEAN DIFFERENCE tells us that the GPA for "Full-Time Employees" is significantly greater than that of "Unemployed" (we derive this since the 5th row of the table has a COLUMN I of "Full Time", a COLUMN J of "Unemployed" and a MEAN DIFFERENCE of .17814, meaning that "Full Time" is larger than "Unemployed" by .17814). As always, be careful with your conclusions beyond this point. You have demonstrated that "Full-time" employees have higher GPAs than their "Unemployed" classmates, but why is a mystery that would warrant future research, and you can certainly suggest possibilities as long as you keep it totally hypothetical and not suggestive.

Now what if the normality assumption did not hold up, or the sample size was relatively small? Then you would use the nonparametric equivalent known as the Kruskal-Wallis test which tests for a difference in the distributions of GPAs for the three Employment groups.

To conduct the Kruskal-Wallis test, go to ANALYZE → NONPARAMETRIC TESTS → LEGACY DIALOGS → K INDEPENDENT SAMPLES. Choose GPA as the TEST VARIABLE, choose Employ as the GROUPING VARIABLE, and check the KRUSKAL-WALLIS H box.

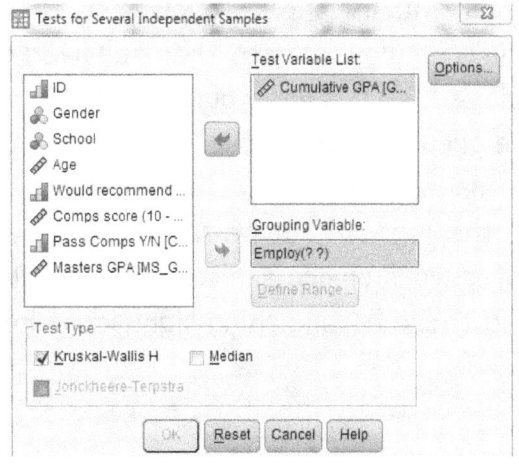

Now choose DEFINE RANGE so that we can tell SPSS where the three groups lie. In this case, the three groups have values of 0, 1 or 2 for "Unemployed", "Part-Time" and "Full-Time" respectively, so enter a range of 0 to 2. Then CONTINUE.

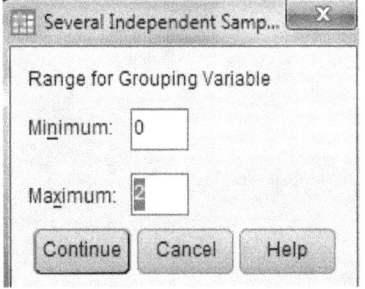

If you would like, you may click OPTIONS and choose DESCRIPTIVE STATISTICS. You already have this information, but sometimes it is great to see whether the format or information provided is different from what you have already seen. Click CONTINUE and OK.

The null hypothesis being tested is that the distribution of GPA's is equal for the three Employment Status groups. The table at the top shows that there were 25 "Unemployed", 45 "Part-Timers", and 130 "Full-Timers". The ASYMP. SIG. value of .014 is less than .05, thus you would reject Ho and conclude a difference in the distribution of GPA by Employment Status. To find the specific difference, look at the MEAN RANKS. "Full-Time Employees" have the highest MEAN RANK, followed by "Part-Time Employees" and then followed by "Unemployed." Thus you would conclude

Ranks

	Employment Status	N	Mean Rank
Cumulative GPA	Unemployed	25	74.20
	Part-Time	45	92.17
	Full-Time	130	108.44
	Total	200	

Test Statistics[a,b]

	Cumulative GPA
Chi-square	8.545
df	2
Asymp. Sig.	.014

a. Kruskal Wallis Test

b. Grouping Variable: Employment Status

that the greater the degree to which a learner is employed, the higher the GPA. Of course this may seem like "Unemployed" are just lazier or "Full-Timer" are doing school work on the job, but maybe the "Unemployed" are parents of toddlers or are actively looking for work or are senior citizens. The point is that you don't know why this is the case, and there is something significant here worth investigating further.

So let's review.

State the hypotheses:
    Ho: There is no difference in the mean GPA for PhD learners as
          a function of their employment status.
    Ha: There is a difference in the mean GPA for PhD learners as a
          function of their employment status.

Choose a significance level → .05

State the assumption(s):
    PhD GPAs are normally distributed.
    → evaluate graphically or with a Kolmogorov-Smirnov test

    The 3 employment groups are independent.
    → must be confirmed by the researcher

    GPAs for Unemployed vs. Part-Timers vs. Full-Timers have equal
        variances.
    → evaluated graphically or with Levene's test
    → ANOVA can handle this assumption being violated.

Conduct One-Way Analysis of Variance

Compare the sig.value / p-value to .05. If greater than .05, do not
reject Ho and then state that there is insufficient evidence to
conclude a difference in the PhD GPAs as a function of a learner's
employment status. If less than .05, reject Ho and conclude that
there is a difference in GPA by Employment Status, then conduct a
Post Hoc test to find the specific differences. Feel free to add
some insights in English, but be careful not to overstate beyond what
you tested.

If the normality assumption does not hold, conduct a Kruskal-Wallis
test with the following hypothesis →
    Ho: there is no difference in the distribution of GPAs for the
        Unemployed vs. Part-Time vs. Full-Time employees.

CHAPTER 10: Chi Square Test of Independence

In this chapter we shall walk through the steps for conducting a Chi Square Test of Independence. For this test, a relationship is tested between two nominal or ordinal variables. It is a perfect test to use with ordinal variables using the Likert scale.

Suppose you wanted to know whether one's recommendation for a PhD program depends on whether the learner passed his/her Comps exam. The null hypothesis (Ho) and alternate hypothesis (Ha) would be:

> Ho: A learner's recommendation for the PhD program is independent of whether he/she passed the Comps exam.
>
> Ha: A learner's recommendation for the PhD program is dependent on whether he/she passed the Comps exam.

The independent variable here is the COMPS result and the dependent variable here is the RECOMMENDATION since we are trying to predict one's RECOMMENDATION from his/her score on the COMPS.

Since we are testing the dependence of one variable on another, we use a Chi Square Test of Independence. To do so, there is an assumption that each observation is independent of the others (that is, a learner can only appear once in the table); this assumption must be confirmed by the researcher.

We need to crosstabulate the data. Go to ANALYZE → DESCRIPTIVE STATISTICS → CROSSTABS

NOTE: you will see that the NONPARAMETRIC TESTS menu has a CHI SQUARE option, but CROSSTABS has far more options available when doing a Test of Independence (there are other Chi Square tests).

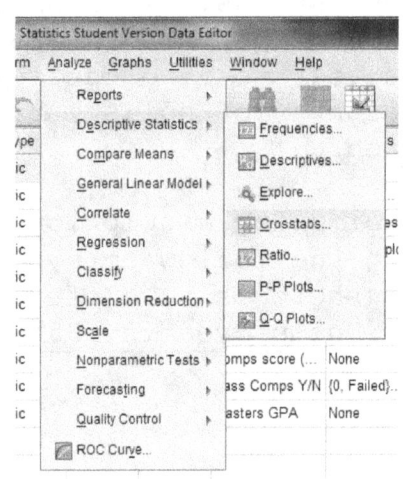

Select Comps_PF for the ROW and Recommend for the COLUMN. Note, it is just a personal preference to put the independent variable in the rows. Now choose CELLS.

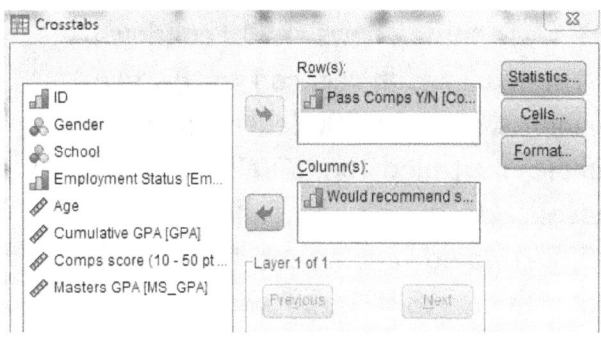

Check the OBSERVED box → this will give us the actual number of learners who passed / failed the Comps and who did / did not recommend the PhD program. Also check the ROW Percentages box → this will tell us of those who passed the Comps, what

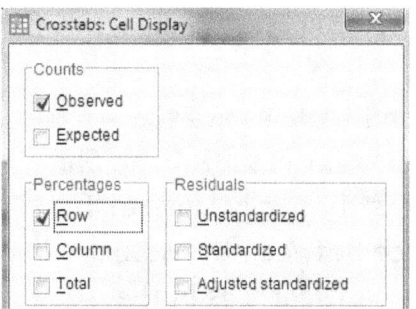

percent did or did not recommend the PhD program, and of those who failed their Comps exam, what percent did or did not recommend the PhD program. Checking the COLUMN Percentages will give you percentages the other way (i.e., of those who recommend the PhD program, how many passed Comps). Checking the TOTAL Percentages gives you percentages of each cell vs. the total (i.e., what percent of the entire sample passed Comps AND recommend the PhD). Feel free to check as many of them as you wish to use, but using all of them makes the table a bit busier, so I recommend running it once, looking at the output, and then rerunning and removing what you really don't want or need. Click CONTINUE. Now choose STATISTICS.

Check the CHI-SQUARE box to compute the Chi Square statistic. Check the LAMBDA box to assess the predictability of the dependent variable (not often used, but let's look at it here). And since the two variables are ordinal, check the GAMMA box so we can see if a direct or inverse relationship exists between the two variables (also not commonly used). Click CONTINUE and OK.

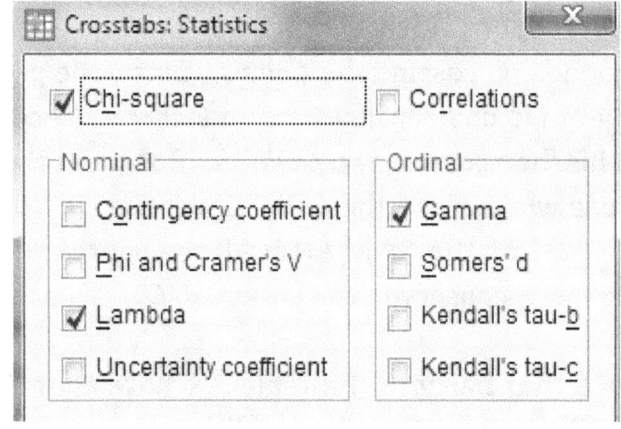

The first table shows the breakdown of the learners in regards to the two variables. Of the 200 learners in the sample, 33 failed the COMPS and 167 passed. Of the 33 who failed, 15 (45.5%) would recommend the PhD program and 18 (54.5%) would not. Of the 167 who passed the COMPS,

Pass Comps Y/N * Would recommend school Crosstabulation

| | | | Would recommend school | | |
			No	Yes	Total
Pass Comps Y/N	Failed	Count	18	15	33
		% within Pass Comps Y/N	54.5%	45.5%	100.0%
	Passed	Count	40	127	167
		% within Pass Comps Y/N	24.0%	76.0%	100.0%
Total		Count	58	142	200
		% within Pass Comps Y/N	29.0%	71.0%	100.0%

127 (76.0%) would recommend the PhD program and 40 (24.0%) would not.

The second table shows the hypothesis test results. The Chi Square test basically looks at the difference between the actual breakdown of learners in the table vs. what is expected if the two variables were independent. Since 71% of the 200 learners

Chi-Square Tests

	Value	df	Asymp. Sig. (2-sided)	Exact Sig. (2-sided)	Exact Sig. (1-sided)
Pearson Chi-Square	12.526[a]	1	.000		
Continuity Correction[b]	11.084	1	.001		
Likelihood Ratio	11.510	1	.001		
Fisher's Exact Test				.001	.001
Linear-by-Linear Association	12.463	1	.000		
N of Valid Cases	200				

a. 0 cells (.0%) have expected count less than 5. The minimum expected count is 9.57.

b. Computed only for a 2x2 table

would recommend the PhD program, a truly independent scenario would have 71% of those who passed the Comps giving their recommendation and 71% of those who failed the Comps giving their recommendation. Chi Square compares the *Actual* vs. the *Expected*, and the larger the Chi Square value, the greater the difference in the two, and the more likely the variables are dependent. In this case, Chi Square = 12.526; while this may not be meaningful in itself, you can just look at the ASYMP. SIG. (2-SIDED) value of .000. If this sig. value / p-value were greater than .05, you would not reject Ho and state that insufficient evidence exists to conclude a learner's recommendation of the PhD program depends on passing the Comps. Since the p-value = .000 which is less than .05, you should reject Ho and conclude that a learner's recommendation of the PhD program does depend on his/her passing the COMPS. Based on the output table, you would even conclude that those who passed the COMPS were more likely to recommend the PhD program. As for the rest of the table, most of the content can be disregarded. FISHER'S EXACT TEST is a more conservative version of Chi Square, but is not often discussed.

Note that beneath the table is a note that "0 cells have expected count less than 5." For the Chi Square test to be valid, most of the cells must have an expected count greater than 5, and none of them can have an expected count less than 1. This table has none less than 5, so it is valid. It is not important to actually display the expected counts, and it is often confusing to display in the output, but if you wish to see it, you could redo the crosstabulation and check the EXPECTED box.

Directional Measures

			Value	Asymp. Std. Error[a]	Approx. T[b]	Approx. Sig.
Nominal by Nominal	Lambda	Symmetric	.033	.062	.523	.601
		Pass Comps Y/N Dependent	.000	.000	.[c]	.[c]
		Would recommend school Dependent	.052	.096	.523	.601
	Goodman and Kruskal tau	Pass Comps Y/N Dependent	.063	.038		.000[d]
		Would recommend school Dependent	.063	.038		.000[d]

In the third table we see the LAMBDA has a value of .033. This means that using one's Comps result to predict one's recommendation would reduce the error in prediction by 3.3%. A value of 0 means that the independent variable is of no help in predicting the dependent variable, and a value of 1 means that it predicts perfectly. This value is clearly not a good one, so a relationship exists, but not one to use for fortune telling. The GOODMAN and KRUSKAL TAU is a modification of LAMBDA.

Symmetric Measures

		Value	Asymp. Std. Error[a]	Approx. T[b]	Approx. Sig.
Ordinal by Ordinal	Gamma	.584	.130	3.040	.002
N of Valid Cases		200			

a. Not assuming the null hypothesis.

b. Using the asymptotic standard error assuming the null hypothesis.

In the fourth table we see the GAMMA has a value of .584. Since both variables are ordinal, we look at the direction of the scales. Comps_PF goes from "Fail" to "Pass" while Recommend goes from "No" to "Yes". A positive GAMMA means that as the Comps_PF increases, the Recommend increases, and a negative GAMMA means that as one increases the other decreases. A value of 1.00 is a perfect positive relationship, and a value of -1.00 is a perfect inverse relationship. Since the APPROX. SIG. is .002 which is less than .05, the GAMMA is significant, and the large value of .584 tells us that passing the Comps increases the likelihood of recommending the PhD program, and failing the Comps increases the likelihood of not recommending the PhD program.

So let's review.

State the hypotheses:
    Ho: A learner's recommendation for the PhD program is
         independent of whether he/she passed the Comps exam.
    Ha: A learner's recommendation for the PhD program is dependent
         on whether he/she passed the Comps exam.

Choose a significance level → .05

State the assumption(s):
    All observations are independent.
    → must be confirmed by the researcher; basically means that each
       learner is only in the data once.

Conduct a Chi Square Test of Independence. Look at the CHI SQUARE
and LAMBDA values. If the two variables are ordinal, look at GAMMA
too.

Compare the Chi Square sig.value / p-value to .05. If greater than
.05, do not reject Ho and then state that there is insufficient
evidence to conclude the learner's recommendation of the PhD program
depends on his/her Comps results. If less than .05, reject Ho and
conclude that the learner's recommendation of the PhD program depends
on his/her Comps results. You can look at the output table to draw
conclusions about which Comps results predict which Recommendation.

Look at the Lambda to determine how predictable the relationship is;
the closer to 1.00, the better the predictability, with scores
ranging from 0 to 1.

Look at the Gamma to determine the direction of the relationship. A
positive Gamma means that as you increase the value on the
independent variable's scale (Comps_PF), you can predict a higher
value on the dependent variable's scale (Recommend); a negative Gamma
means that they move in opposite directions. Disregard the Gamma
unless both variables are ordinal.

CHAPTER 11: Hypothesis Test for Correlation

In this chapter we shall walk through the steps for conducting a Test of Correlation. For this test, a relationship is tested between two scale variables (one independent and one dependent).

Suppose you wanted to know whether there is a relationship between one's GPA and his/her COMPS score. The null hypothesis (Ho) and alternate hypothesis (Ha) would be:

Ho: There is no correlation between GPA and COMPS score (i.e., correlation = 0).
Ha: There is a correlation between GPA and COMPS score.

The independent variable here is GPA and the dependent variable is the COMPS since we are trying to predict COMPS scores from GPA. This variable designation arises from our understanding that GPA precedes taking the comprehensive examination from a chronological perspective.

Since we are measuring the relationship between two scale variables, we use a test of Correlation. To do so, there are a few assumptions we need to consider:

> The GPAs and COMPS scores are normally distributed (this was addressed in Chapter 2, but we need to look at the COMPS scores)
> All observations are independent of each other (meaning that each learner's GPA and COMPS are not related to another learner's). This assumption cannot be tested, so it is up to the researcher to confirm this fact.
> The variance of COMPS scores is the same across all GPAs (this is very difficult to test, so we just rely on the test for normality).
> There is a linear relationship between GPA and COMPS (if it doesn't appear linear graphically, there is no point in proceeding since you could get misleading results).

First let's look at the graph to see if a linear relationship might exist. Select GRAPHS → LEGACY DIALOGS → SCATTER/DOT.

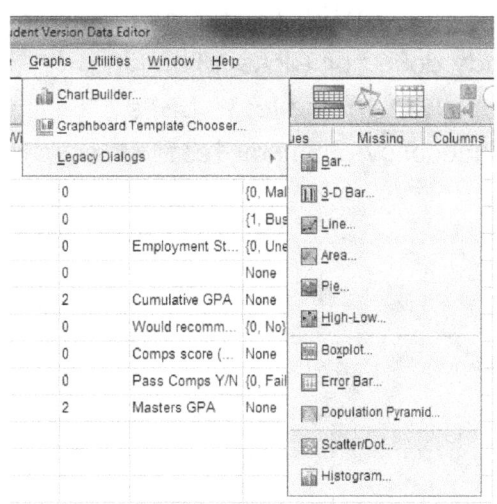

Then select SIMPLE SCATTER and DEFINE.

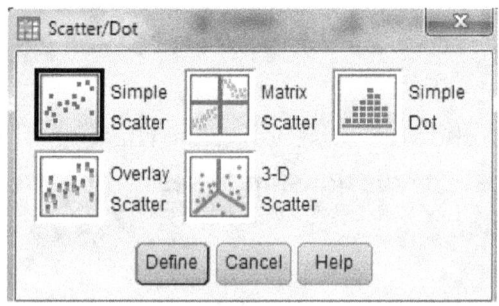

Choose the dependent variable <u>Comps</u> for the Y-AXIS and the independent variable <u>GPA</u> for the X-AXIS.
Click OK.

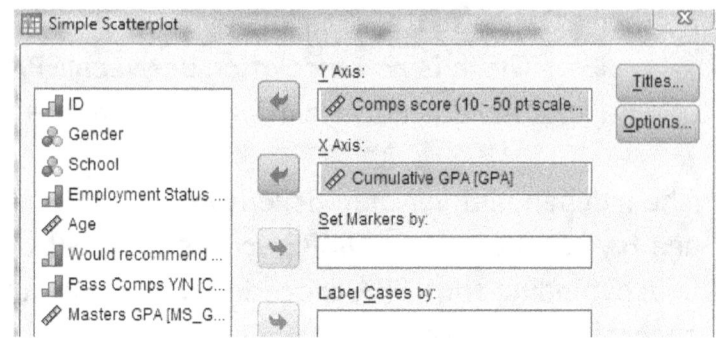

The dots appear to have a linear pattern where increasing GPAs correspond to increasing Comps scores. If you would like to add a line to this graph, double click on it and go to the CHART EDITOR.

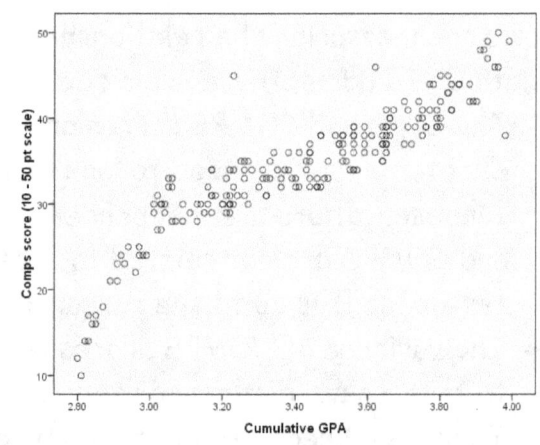

As shown in chapter 7, you can create a histogram for the COMPS scores as you have already done for GPAs. This pattern looks skewed to the left. Let's look at the Kolmogorov-Smirnov test.

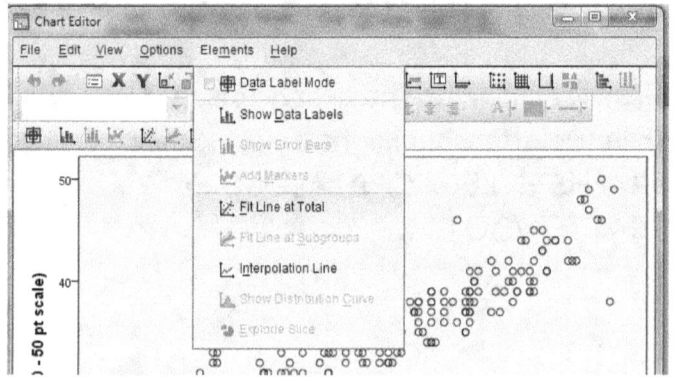

From the PROPERTIES menu, choose
LINEAR and then CLOSE.

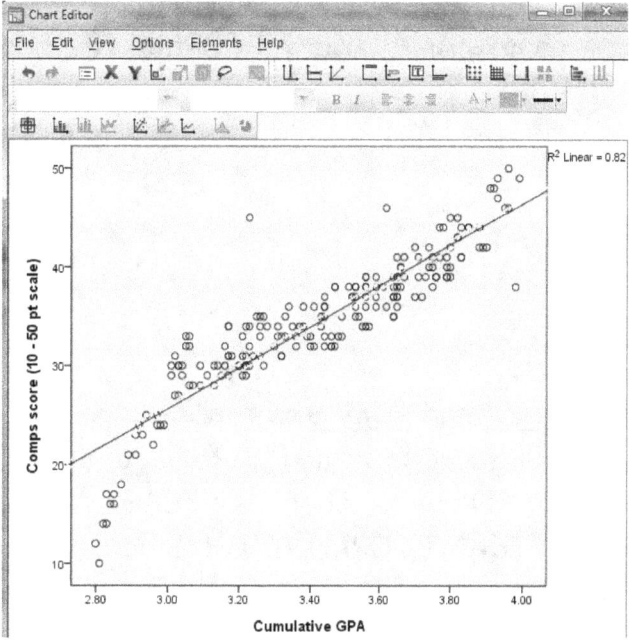

You now have the required scatterplot
and regression line. Click on the X in
the upper right corner to close the
CHART EDITOR and return to the
output file.

As shown in chapter 6, you can create
a histogram for the Comps scores as
you have already done for GPAs. This
pattern looks skewed to the left. So
let's look at the Kolmogorov-Smirnov
test.

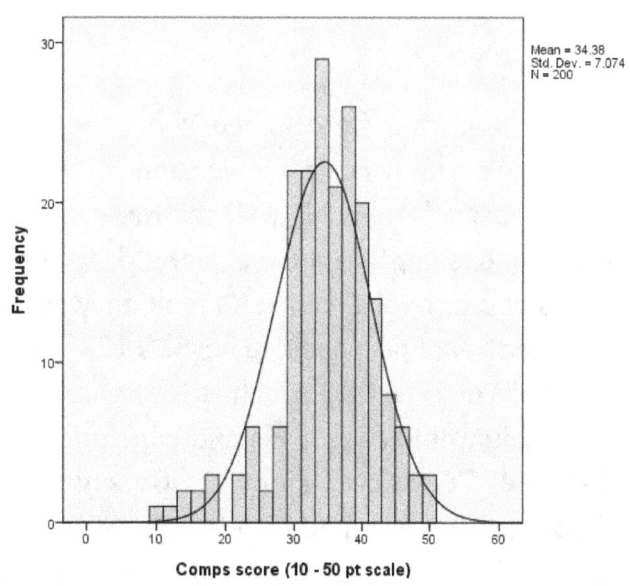

The ASYMP. SIG. (2-TAILED) of .029 is less than .05, so we would reject the assumption of normality. This means we cannot conduct the parametric test, but we shall do it here for educational purposes only.

One-Sample Kolmogorov-Smirnov Test

		Comps score (10 - 50 pt scale)
N		200
Normal Parameters[a,b]	Mean	34.38
	Std. Deviation	7.074
Most Extreme Differences	Absolute	.103
	Positive	.057
	Negative	-.103
Kolmogorov-Smirnov Z		1.455
Asymp. Sig. (2-tailed)		.029

a. Test distribution is Normal.

b. Calculated from data.

To conduct the Pearson Correlation test, choose ANALYZE → CORRELATE → BIVARIATE.

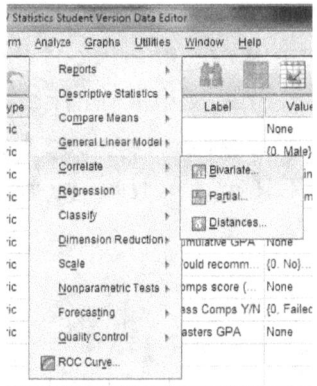

Select <u>GPA</u> and <u>COMPS</u> as the VARIABLES. Check the PEARSON and SPEARMAN boxes. Check the FLAG SIGNIFICANT CORRELATIONS box. Then OK.

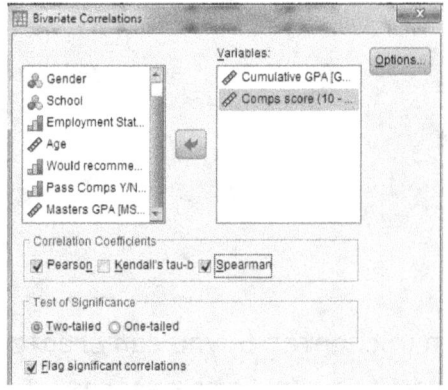

This is the output for the Pearson correlation, the parametric version of the test for correlation. Now since the normality assumption was not upheld, these results are not valid, but let's look anyway for educational purposes. The SIG (2-TAILED) value is .000 which is less than

Correlations

		Cumulative GPA	Comps score (10 - 50 pt scale)
Cumulative GPA	Pearson Correlation	1	.905**
	Sig. (2-tailed)		.000
	N	200	200
Comps score (10 - 50 pt scale)	Pearson Correlation	.905**	1
	Sig. (2-tailed)	.000	
	N	200	200

**. Correlation is significant at the 0.01 level (2-tailed).

.05, so you would reject Ho and conclude a correlation exists. The PEARSON CORRELATION Coefficient is .905 which is strong (.70 to 1.00 is considered "Strong", .30 to .69 is considered "Moderate", and below .30 is considered "Weak"). This means that as GPA increases, Comps scores increase very predictably.

Now let's look at the Spearman Rank Correlation results, the nonparametric version that doesn't depend on normal distributions. This is the output for the Spearman Rank Correlation. The SIG. (2-TAILED) value is .000 which is less than .05, so you would reject Ho and conclude a correlation exists. The SPEARMAN RANK CORRELATION Coefficient is .931 which is strong. This means that as GPA increases, Comps scores increase very predictably.

Correlations

			Cumulative GPA	Comps score (10 - 50 pt scale)
Spearman's rho	Cumulative GPA	Correlation Coefficient	1.000	.931**
		Sig. (2-tailed)	.	.000
		N	200	200
	Comps score (10 - 50 pt scale)	Correlation Coefficient	.931**	1.000
		Sig. (2-tailed)	.000	.
		N	200	200

**. Correlation is significant at the 0.01 level (2-tailed).

Usually researchers want more than just the correlation results – they want to explain the relationship and do more with it. Let's look at Regression, which goes along with Correlation but here we get to determine the equation of the line in the scatterplot (which then allows you to do forecasting). Go to ANALYZE → REGRESSION → LINEAR

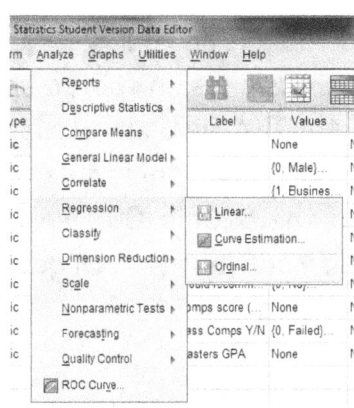

Choose Comps as the DEPENDENT variable and GPA as the independent variable (note that we can enter several independent variables if doing Multiple Regression, but Simple Regression requires only one). Now click on STATISTICS.

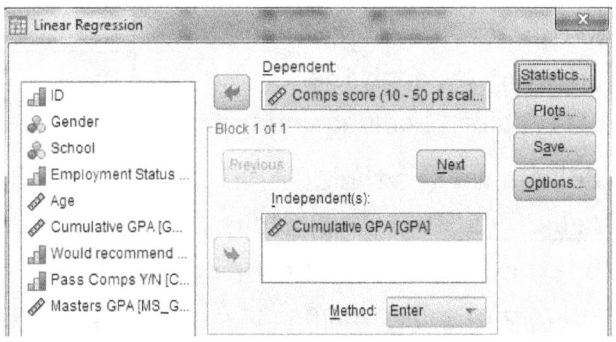

The defaults that are checked are good. You want the ESTIMATES and the MODEL FIT. The others aren't necessary here, especially with SIMPLE REGRESSION, but feel free to try them all out. Click CONTINUE and OK.

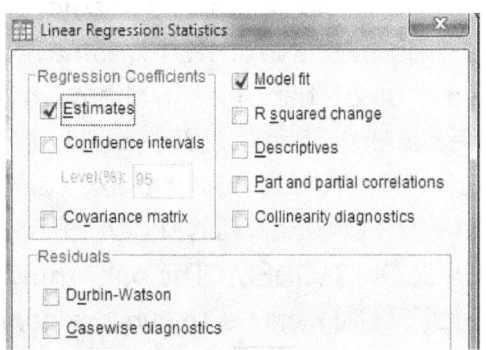

In this first table we see that the Correlation (R) is .905, indicating that there is a strong positive correlation between the two variables. The

Model Summary

Model	R	R Square	Adjusted R Square	Std. Error of the Estimate
1	.905[a]	.820	.819	3.013

a. Predictors: (Constant), Cumulative GPA

Coefficient of Determination (R SQUARE) of .820 tells us that 82.0% of the variability in the dependent variable (Comps) can be explained by the regression equation (which in this case consists of just the one independent variable, GPA). A perfect correlation of 1.00 would have an R-Squared of 100% since one variable explains the changes in the other perfectly.

The second table is an ANOVA table because Regression is, in fact, a special case of an ANOVA problem. It is not critical to understand this table except to note that the SIG. is .000 which is clearly significant (but we can get this from the next table).

ANOVA[b]

Model		Sum of Squares	df	Mean Square	F	Sig.
1	Regression	8160.103	1	8160.103	899.101	.000[a]
	Residual	1797.017	198	9.076		
	Total	9957.120	199			

a. Predictors: (Constant), Cumulative GPA

b. Dependent Variable: Comps score (10 - 50 pt scale)

This third table is the real prize. We get to see the equation of the Regression Line that went through the Scatterplot. Looking under the

Coefficients[a]

Model		Unstandardized Coefficients		Standardized Coefficients	t	Sig.
		B	Std. Error	Beta		
1	(Constant)	-36.660	2.379		-15.411	.000
	Cumulative GPA	20.763	.692	.905	29.985	.000

a. Dependent Variable: Comps score (10 - 50 pt scale)

B column we see the COEFFICIENTS of -36.66 for the CONSTANT and 20.763 for the Cumulative GPA. This means that the Regression Equation (also known as a Regression Model) is "Comps = -36.66 + 20.763 * GPA". The coefficient of 20.763 means that a one grade point improvement in GPA translates to a 20.763 improvement in Comps score. So a GPA of 3.00 would result in a predicted Comps score of -36.66 + 20.763 * 3.00 = -36.66 + 62.289 = 25.629. Note that it is never a good idea to input a value outside the range of data (so if all of the GPAs in the data set that were used to create the Regression Model were between 1.50 and 3.25, you shouldn't try to do a prediction with a GPA less than 1.50 or greater than 3.25. Notice how you could have used the REGRESSION option and gotten your CORRELATION COEFFICIENTS, the SIGNIFICANCE LEVEL and a bonus REGRESSION MODEL. The only thing you can't do here that you could do in the CORRELATION menu is to run the nonparametric SPEARMAN RANK test.

So let's review.

```
State the hypotheses:
     Ho:  There is no correlation between GPA and Comps score (i.e.,
          correlation = 0).
     Ha:  There is a correlation between GPA and Comps score.

Choose a significance level → .05

State the assumption(s):
     PhD GPAs and Comps scores are normally distributed.
     → evaluate graphically or with a Kolmogorov-Smirnov test

     The observations of GPAs and Comps scores are independent.
     → must be confirmed by the researcher

     Variance of the dependent variable (Comps) is the same across
          all values of the independent variable (GPA).
     → difficult to test, so we rely on the normality assumption.

     There is a linear relationship between the two variables.
     → evaluate graphically with a scatterplot

Conduct a Test of Correlation
     → Pearson if normality assumption is upheld, Spearman if not

Compare the sig.value / p-value to .05.  If greater than .05, do not
reject Ho and then state that there is insufficient evidence to
conclude a correlation exists between the GPA and Comps scores.  If
less than .05, reject Ho and conclude that there is a correlation
between GPA and Comps, then assess the strength of the correlation
coefficient (.70 - 1.00 = strong, .30 - .69 = moderate, less than .30
= weak).

And while you are at it, conduct a Regression Analysis to determine
the Regression Equation.
```

CHAPTER 12: Multiple Regression Analysis

In this chapter we shall walk through the steps for conducting a Multiple Regression Analysis, which is what you would do when you have 2 or more variables used to predict a single variable. The object here is to create the best equation / model for forecasting by eliminating variables that are not significant and don't contribute much toward the value of the predicted / dependent variable. If you were trying to create a model for estimating the selling price of homes, you might look at the age of the home, the location, the size, the building material, the number of bedrooms and bathrooms, whether it has a pool or garage, and its general location. Some of these are clearly better predictors than others, but some are still valuable contributors to the overall prediction. Multiple Regression will help to determine the relationships of the variables and the best fitting model with the variables provided. Let's look at creating a model to predict one's Comps score using Gender, Age, PhD GPA and MS GPA. Note that we can actually use a categorical / nominal variable like Gender providing it has only two values (if it has more than two, it would require creating a dummy variable for each value, but that is beyond the scope of this book).

Go to ANALYZE → REGRESSION → LINEAR. Choose <u>Comps</u> as the DEPENDENT variable. Then choose <u>Gender</u>, <u>Age</u>, <u>GPA</u> and <u>MS_GPA</u> as the INDEPENDENT variables. In the METHOD dropdown menu, choose BACKWARD (this method puts all of the variables in and then removes one non-significant variable at a time

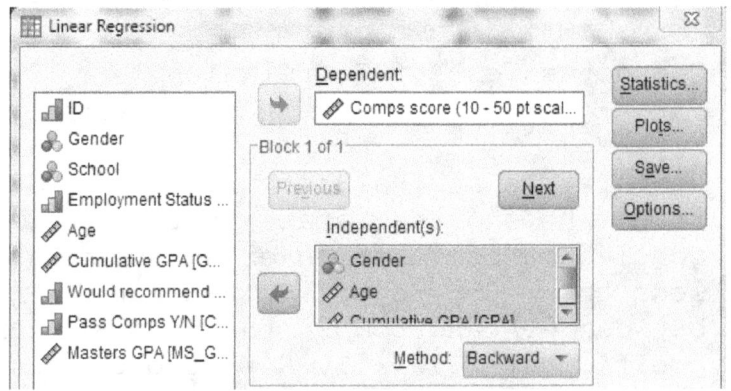

(starting with the highest SIG. value), until only significant variables remain. Click on STATISTICS.

Keep the two defaults (ESTIMATES and MODEL FIT) and also add R SQUARED CHANGE. The PARTIAL CORRELATIONS and COLLINEARITY DIAGNOSTICS are a bit more complex and beyond the scope of this book (but more advanced analysis may require your using them). Click CONTINUE and OK.

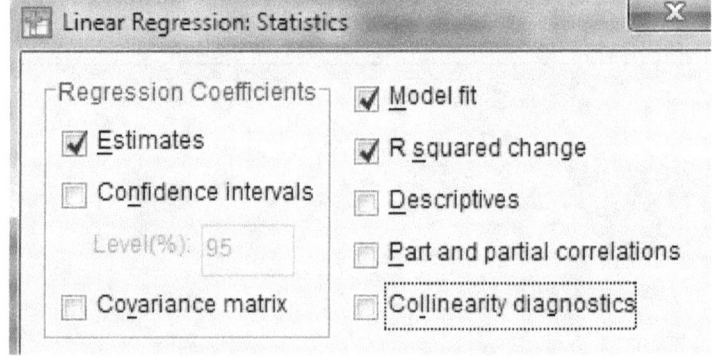

In this first table, we see that in the MODEL 1, all four independent variables were loaded. In MODEL 2, Age was removed and the other three variables remained. Since that is the last model, it indicates that the remaining variables were significant. Let's continue.

Variables Entered/Removed[b]

Model	Variables Entered	Variables Removed	Method
1	Masters GPA, Age, Gender, Cumulative GPA[a]	.	Enter
2	.	Age	Backward (criterion: Probability of F-to-remove >= .100).

a. All requested variables entered.

b. Dependent Variable: Comps score (10 - 50 pt scale)

Model Summary

Model	R	R Square	Adjusted R Square	Std. Error of the Estimate	Change Statistics				
					R Square Change	F Change	df1	df2	Sig. F Change
1	.947[a]	.897	.895	2.290	.897	426.111	4	195	.000
2	.947[b]	.897	.896	2.284	.000	.052	1	195	.820

a. Predictors: (Constant), Masters GPA, Age, Gender, Cumulative GPA

b. Predictors: (Constant), Masters GPA, Gender, Cumulative GPA

In this second table we see the statistics for each of the two models. The first model had a CORRELATION COEFFICIENT of .947 (very strong). The second model had an identical CORRELATION COEFFICIENT of .947, which means that removing Age had no impact on the bottom line (it essentially did not contribute to the predicting of the Comps score). The R SQUARE CHANGE shows a value of .000 which is the difference in the correlations as we go from one model to the next. What Stepwise Regression does is to eliminate variables that contribute so little to the relationship that they are not worth keeping (i.e., wouldn't you rather predict the price of a house with 90% accuracy using 3 variables vs. predicting with 91% accuracy using 10 variables?).

Let's skip the ANOVA table this time and move to the fourth table. Here we see the COEFFICIENTS of the variables, enabling us to write out the Regression Equation. Since we want to use the best model, we shall go to the last one (i.e., MODEL 2). Note that in MODEL 1, all of the SIG. values were less than .05 except <u>Age</u>, which had .820. If any are above .05, the largest is removed and the Regression is run again.

Coefficients[a]

Model		Unstandardized Coefficients		Standardized Coefficients	t	Sig.
		B	Std. Error	Beta		
1	(Constant)	-44.738	2.167		-20.645	.000
	Gender	1.412	.345	.100	4.091	.000
	Age	.004	.018	.005	.228	.820
	Cumulative GPA	5.219	1.401	.228	3.726	.000
	Masters GPA	17.128	1.477	.700	11.599	.000
2	(Constant)	-44.561	2.018		-22.082	.000
	Gender	1.399	.340	.099	4.118	.000
	Cumulative GPA	5.218	1.397	.228	3.735	.000
	Masters GPA	17.131	1.473	.700	11.630	.000

a. Dependent Variable: Comps score (10 - 50 pt scale)

So the Regression Equation here is
"Comps = -44.561 + 1.399 * Gender + 5.218 * GPA + 17.131 * MS_GPA"
If a Male with a 3.50 PhD GPA and 3.00 Masters GPA took the Comps, we would predict his score to be -44.561 + 1.399 *0 + 5.218 * 3.50 + 17.131 * 3.00 = -44.561 + 0 + 18.263 + 51.393 = 25.095.

The coefficients have meaning too. The 1.399 for Gender means that Females are predicted to score 1.399 more than Males (note that the value for Gender is 0 for males and 1 for females). 5.218 implies that one grade point improvement in PhD GPA translates to a 5.218 improvement in Comps. And the 17.131 means that one grade point improvement in MS GPA translates to a 17.131 improvement in Comps.

If you wonder why we don't just remove all non-significant variables at once, it is due to a concept known as collinearity. Sometimes two variables are significant but are related to each other strongly, and as such, they cancel each other out in the correlation. Going back to the Real Estate example, imagine if one variable were the size of a house in square feet and another variable was the size of a house in square meters. These two variables are perfectly correlated (because one is essentially a translation of the other with different units). House size is a significant predictor of sales price, but these two variables will battle each other to see which is superior, and they will both lose. If each individually were moderately correlated to sales price, together they are both going to show as non-significant. If we eliminate one of them from the model, the other suddenly shows itself as significant and you lose nothing since both variables are basically the same anyway. So the BACKWARD STEPWISE REGRESSION method helps to protect you from erroneously throwing out a significant variable. And since it takes collinearity into account with its procedure, we needn't delve into the other collinearity statistics at this time.

Well that wraps up the most common statistical tests, probably appearing in over 98% of quantitative or mixed-methods dissertations. Whether your variables are nominal, ordinal or scale, and whether you are testing one, two or more samples doesn't matter, as there is a test for almost any combination. You just need to know the right one to use, how to set it up, and how to interpret the results. Hopefully this book will help you realize that you CAN do this without hiring a statistician. You will feel better about yourself and your research study if you do it yourself, but don't hesitate to get a tutor. SPSS is a powerful vehicle; you don't need to know how to build it, but you should learn to drive it. Good luck!